Jean Rhys

LONGMAN GROUP LIMITED
LONDON

Associated companies, branches and
representatives throughout the world

First published 1978

ISBN 0 582 78505.7

Printed in Great Britain by
Lowe & Brydone Printers Limited, Thetford

Critical Studies of Caribbean Writers
General Editor: Mervyn Morris

Jean Rhys

Louis James

Longman

Acknowledgements and Dedication

Mervyn Morris first suggested that I write this book, and became its scrupulous and creative editor. Jean Rhys gave unfailing and most generous help. The many others who made this small book possible include, in England, Tristan Powell and Francis Wyndham; in the West Indies, Phyllis and Charles Allfrey, Father R. Proesmans, C.Ss.R., Thomas Joseph of the Roseau Archives, Elsie Royer, Elsie Ritchie, and Gordon Rohlehr. To all these my sincerest thanks. I would like in particular to dedicate this book to Phyllis Allfrey, who has given so much to West Indian life and literature.

LOUIS JAMES

Contents

Abbreviations

One
The Girl from the Island

'There are places which are supposed to be hostile to human beings and to know how to defend themselves. When I was a child it used to be said that this island was one of them.'[1] The child was Gwen Williams, later to become Jean Rhys, and the island was her childhood Dominica. Dominica, so called because Columbus visited it first on a Sunday in 1493, was once the highest mountain in a range enclosing the Caribbean Sea. It is now the most rugged of all the Caribbean islands. Although only twenty-nine miles long by sixteen broad, its peaks rise to more than five thousand feet; for its size, it is more mountainous than Switzerland. It is a land of violent contrasts. Crags, pierced with waterfalls and racing rivers, give way to shallow, park-like valleys. One emerges from the densest vegetation into the Valley of Desolation, a bare gorge swept by sulphur fumes from the Boiling Lake, a small geyser in a volcanic crater. The rainfall – in the interior one of the highest in the world – and the rich black volcanic soil produce an overwhelming green. Travelling the islands, Alec Waugh wrote of Dominica, 'I had never thought of green as being a colour that could dazzle you.'[2]

Yet the island remained largely hostile to settlers. Communications were, and are, difficult. Thomas Atwood wrote of roads, in the eighteenth century, 'in general dug in the sides of mountains of stupendous heights above the rivers or sea, the billows of which are continually dashing at the feet of them in a frightful manner.'[3] Dominica was the last refuge of the Caribs, protected by the mountains on one side, and the violence of the Atlantic surges on the other. Their settlements still remain in the Salybia reserve to the north-east of the island, although with the new road no longer cut off from the rest of the island. The interior could hide, in the eighteenth and nineteenth centuries, whole villages of runaway slaves, who emerged to harry the white plantations. Plantation life itself was hard and insecure. 'You are getting along fine,' wrote Jean Rhys, 'and then a hurricane comes, or a disease of the crops that nobody can cure, and there you are – more West Indian ruins and labour lost. It has been going on for more than three hundred years.'[4] Its troubled history will be looked at later, but Dominica has remained one of the least developed of the Caribbean islands.

Towards the end of the nineteenth century William Rhys Williams, the son of a Welsh Anglican clergyman, came to the island as a doctor. It was perhaps his temperament that drew him to settle on the wildest of the Leeward islands. As a boy of fourteen he had tried to run away to sea from his home in Caernarfon, and had got as far as Cardiff. After this his father had let him train on the sailing ship *Worcester*. Later he went to medical school, and then travelled the world as a ship's doctor. He took a house at the upper end of the little town, on the corner of Cork and St Mary's streets, still within view of the sea. It still stands today, a two-storey house of wood, with slatted shutters to keep out the sun but let in the breeze. The sitting room could hold a small dance. It was built round a yard. At one corner of the yard were two stables for his horses and trap; down the side of the yard, facing the house, was his surgery. His patients were treated like one of his family – whether white or black; he became one of theirs.

For Dr Williams threw himself into the life of Dominica with a lack of reserve and social distinction. He was popular with all sections of the community but some of the more 'respectable' Dominicans thought he did not preserve strictly enough the status of a white doctor in Roseau. Dr Williams enjoyed playing chess, and socialising with both rich and poor. He was very different from Dr

Henry Nicholls whose surgery was across the street. When he treated black people, some said, he kept his gloves on. Later he received a knighthood for his services to the community. But Dr Williams would not have wanted a knighthood if he had been offered one. He drove his horse and trap with verve round the narrow streets, and beyond to the neighbouring communities of Massacre, Loubière, Point Michel, or up winding tracks to Beaubois, to Pachoute where the sulphur fumes from the springs mingled with the scent of ginger lilies as the morning sun caught the peak of Morne Macaque up beyond. It was beautiful; it could also be cruel. Violence had not ended with slavery. In the lonely communities, rum was cheap and machetes were sharp. It could have been one of her father's experiences that Jean Rhys made Christophine describe in *Wide Sargasso Sea*:

> One night . . . I hold on a woman's nose because her husband nearly chop it off with his machete. I hold it on, I send a boy running for the doctor and the doctor come galloping at dead of night to sew up the woman . . . 'Why don't you keep the damn machete in the other room?' he says. They have two small rooms only so I say, 'No doctor – it much worse near the bed. They chop each other up in no time at all.' The doctor he laugh and laugh. Oh he was a good doctor.[5]

Dr Williams married Minna Lockhart, daughter of James Potter Lockhart, who was cousin to John Gibson Lockhart the biographer of Sir Walter Scott. They had five children – Edward, Owen, Minny, Gwen and Brenda. Gwen – later to call herself Jean Rhys – was shy, oversensitive, and often ill. She was the odd one out, overshadowed by her two lively brothers – the three eldest left home when Gwen was still a child – and the vivacious youngest daughter Brenda. She was largely ignored by her mother, who was cold and reserved by temperament, and who preferred the company of the boys. Visitors to the house tended to find Brenda in charge.

The family regime was repressive. Jean was to remember as a child playing a singing game called 'Loobi Li' in Roseau Botanical Gardens 'in all innocence', until fiercely quizzed by her mother, 'Who started it? Who taught you the words?' And the children stopped playing 'Loobi Li', knowing that 'some man or woman – impossible to know – had watched us playing, then gone away to report that we played disgusting games, sang disgusting songs . . .'[6]

From an early age, Gwen had a sense of rejection, and found the outside world different, insensitive. Later she would look back and write, 'I am a well-behaved little girl . . . Too well-behaved . . . I long to be like Other People! The extraordinary, ungetatable, oddly cruel Other People, with their way of wantonly hurting and then accusing you of being thin-skinned, sulky, vindictive or ridiculous.' But however hard she tried, she did not seem able to please. The adult world scolded: 'I am speaking to you; do you not hear? You must break yourself of your habit of never listening. You have such an absent-minded expression. Try not to look vague . . .' The grown-ups in fact were unaware of all the child *was* seeing and hearing. But without recognition, the child felt guilty, a failure. Only her father recognised the appeal for help in the baffled gaze. He praised her cocktail-mixing. Suddenly the little ritual took on the huge significance of being accepted. 'I measure out angostura and gin, feeling important and happy.'[7]

Her father, with his red moustache and his own sad moods, she adored, and he recognised in her his own frustrations. He would suddenly kiss her, hugging her and leaving her breathless. On moonlit nights he would go out boating, and took Gwen with him. In calm, it could be a scene of eldritch beauty, though underlain, for the nervous girl, with menace. 'Then you would imagine the barracoutas – hundreds of them – swimming by the side of the boat, waiting to snap. Flat-headed, sharp-toothed, swimming along the cold white roads the moon makes on the water.'[8] Sometimes it was rough. Then her father was happiest, but Gwen would be terrified and sometimes sick. One night she was not sick at sea, but later, while reading an account of a storm, retched violently. Already she was becoming aware of the interplay of present and remembered worlds that was to form the basis of her fiction.[9]

From an early age she retreated into her own world. The scents, colours and moods of the island filled her sensibility. In the early morning the sea was a 'very tender blue, like the dress of the Virgin Mary, and on it were little white triangles. The fishing boats.' By midday the sea could only be looked at by screwing up the eyes for the glitter. 'Everything was still and languid, worshipping the sun.' When the sun slipped below the sea, night came suddenly, 'a warm, velvety, sweet-smelling night, but frightening and disturbing if one is alone in the hammock.'[10] Her nurse Meta added to the intuitive fear of the other world of the night. She must not sleep in the moon. 'The negroes in general,' wrote Thomas Atwood of Dominica, 'are much addicted to witchcraft and idolatry, both of which seem inherent in them.'[11] The impact of the missionaries, Roman Catholic and Methodist, diffused but never supplanted the traditional beliefs in *obeah*, and the sensitive child was surrounded by its intimations. Meta terrified her with tales of jumbies, *soucoyants* (vampires), and of great spiders that would creep above the sleeping child and drop onto its face. Gwen never lost her fear of insects, or her superstitious sense. Her imaginative awareness of *obeah* was to enable her to create the most hallucinatory scenes of *Wide Sargasso Sea*.

But she was aware of the black community in other ways than through fear. In two of her novels she portrays what it could mean to a reserved, sensitive child, growing up in a largely unresponsive white world concerned with money problems and the narrow social rounds of expatriate group. By comparison the black community seemed to be laughter, singing; it had its folk-tales and masquerades; it accepted life, including sex, with a freedom foreign to the whites. Modern stereotypes of West Indian societies tend to present a simple over-dramatic picture of white against black. Particularly on smaller islands such as Dominica, this is a myth that simplifies and can distort our understanding of what Jean Rhys is writing in her novels. As she herself has protested, 'As far as I can remember, many of the white people did their best [for the racial situation], *leur petit possible* . . . they were not monsters, verging on tyrants, that they are now supposed to have been . . .'[12] The young Gwen was strongly drawn to the black community. Both Anna Morgan in *Voyage in the Dark* and Antoinette Cosway in *Wide Sargasso Sea* reach out towards friendship with black girls. Anna thought 'being black is warm and gay, being white is cold and sad,' and again, 'I wanted to be black. I always wanted to be black.'[13] In the later novel the warmth is felt towards the black nurse Christophine and the peasant girl Tia.

The novels are fiction, but Jean Rhys' empathy is not. Later, lonely in a Paris café, she was suddenly to feel at home when seeing two black men and a mulatto girl, gay, naked under her bright red dress. 'It was because these were my compatriots that in that

Montparnasse restaurant I remembered the Antilles.'[14] But in life and in the fiction there was also the inevitable exclusion from a culture by the tragic Caribbean history of racial division. Anna knew 'that of course [Francine, the black kitchen girl] disliked me too because I was white; and that I would never be able to explain to her that I hated being white. Being white and getting like Hester [her aunt], and all the things you get – old and sad and everything.'[15]

Her father built a holiday house high in the hills above the village of Massacre. Here the long verandah, with the hammock, the three chairs, and the telescope on four legs overlooking the sea were to remain with Gwen to be revisited, as Dickens' childhood world was revisited, in the most vivid moments of her fiction. The telescope recurs three times. It is a vivid personal detail; but it may also have a symbolic significance. It was a lookout from the island towards the comings and goings of the world beyond – 'the French mail on its way to Guadeloupe, the Canadian, the Royal Mail, which should have been stately and was actually the shabbiest of the lot . . . Or an exciting stranger!'[16]

One stranger from the outside world was a touring Cuban circus that set up its little marquee in Roseau. To the excited child the tent was a cathedral; the trapeze, lit with acetylene lamps, impossibly high and perilous. The stars were the Rodriguez family. The highest, most dangerous act was Madame Rodriguez, 'pale, sad and mournful under her make-up,' wearing pink or red tights, swinging at the very top of the tent while the drums rolled and rolled. But the star of all for Gwen was not Madame or Monsieur, but the black-clad, black-eyed, golden-haired Nina Rodriguez, 'the Only Girl Who Works Without a Net.' 'We craned our necks to watch her, a black and gold butterfly caught in a web, weaving in and out of the web, miraculously escaping, miraculously coming to earth again, giving two little stylized hops, smiling, kissing her hands to us.'[17] It was Gwen's first experience of theatre. It was not to be her last.

Apart from such excitements, there was little diversion or cultural life for the growing girl. Little Pointe à Pitre across the sea on Guadeloupe, was Paris to the provincial Roseau. Isolated and poor, Dominica did not have the literary circles found on Barbados and Trinidad, or even some of the smaller islands such as St Lucia and St Kitts. The newspapers at the end of the nineteenth century were sheets whose literacy Jean Rhys was to satirise in the person of Papa Dom of the *Dominica Herald and Leeward Islands Gazette*, who attacked an opponent:

> How far is such a man removed from the ideals of true gentility, from the beautiful description of a contemporary, possibly, though not certainly, the Marquis of Montrose, left us by Shakespeare, the divine poet and genius.
> *'He was a very gentle, perfect knight.'* [18]

In a moving story, 'The Day They Burned the Books', Jean Rhys sketched the kind of isolation faced by a 'literary' figure on the island. Mr Sawyer lives off private means with his mulatto wife, in a house full of his books. It is a conflict of ways of life, of mental worlds. He resents and insults his illiterate wife, and she, silently, resents him. After his death her hatred explodes in a ritual burning of his books. She leaves on one side those whose bindings make them saleable, except when the writer is a woman. She throws a leather-bound Christina Rossetti into the flames, and 'by a flicker in Mrs Sawyer's eyes I knew that worse than men who wrote books were women who wrote books – infinitely worse.' [19]

Yet Gwen – a girl who was to write books – was lucky. She had the use of her father's library which fed her romantic tastes – Byron's *Don Juan*, Milton's *Paradise Lost* (she identified with Satan), Shelley, Keats, the heady stories of the Brontës, of Scott, and Shakespeare – although Shakespeare was to be spoilt by school. Here, too, however, she was fortunate. At an early age she went to the Convent of the Faithful Virgin in Roseau, where schooling was not strenuous either intellectually or in religion. There was little attempt to proselytise the pupils, and the main object was to teach needlework and the other skills required when the girls became – as was their estate in life – young wives. But Gwen had as a teacher one Mother Sacred Heart who had a passionate love of English literature, and found an apt pupil in the doctor's daughter. Mother Sacred Heart, more than any one else, laid the limited but deep foundation of her literary world. [20]

Books were a telescope. Through them she looked to England, a place of long hot summers and abrupt changes into the snows of winter. England had the wide dimensions of the Brontës' Yorkshire fells, and the beauty of Keats' odes. Giant figures – Rob

Roy, Heathcliff, Don Juan – stalked its mountains and its green plains. Dominica was beautiful, but its beauty was like one's hair or clothes, too close to be seen until mirrored by distance. England waited with the wonder of a land to be experienced; a world also of writers and plays and cultured society. In Dominica, after school, there would be marriage and children, the circumscribed life of an island wife, 'being white and getting like Hester, and all the things you get – old and sad and everything.'[21] It would be intolerable.

In 1910, when Gwen was sixteen, preparing for her Cambridge Certificate exams, her maternal aunt visited the island from England. Gwen announced that she wanted to go to England with her aunt. The family were horrified. What would she do in England? Besides, the sea fare was expensive. But her father, who knew what it was to run away to sea, supported her. She was to go to school in England, at Cambridge, and her father would send money for fees and her upkeep. The trunk was packed, and half in a dream the sixteen-year-old who had never seen beyond Dominica kissed her family goodbye before the boat journey through the gentle surf to the waiting steamer. She was to recreate a similar moment for Anna in her novel *Voyage in the Dark*.

> It was when I looked back from the boat and saw the lights of the town bobbing up and down that was the first time I really knew I was going. Uncle Bob said well you're off now and I turned my head so that nobody would see me crying – it ran down my face and splashed into the sea like the rain was splashing – Adieu sweetheart adieu – and I watched the lights heaving up and down.[22]

It was twenty-five years before she was to see Dominica again,[23] and then the island was to be estranged not only by rapid developments on the island itself, but by a life of experience and suffering that had changed Gwen from the girl who stood on the long verandah peering through the telescope.

Notes

1. 'T.P.', p. 81
2. Alec Waugh, quoted in Basil Cracknell, *Dominica*, 1974, p. 24
3. T. Atwood, *History of the Island of Dominica*, 1791, pp. 283–4
4. 'T.P.', p. 81
5. *W.S.S.* p. 125
6. Jean Rhys, *My Day*, 1975, pp. 16–18
7. *T.B.L.*, pp. 163–5
8. *V.I.D.*, p. 46
9. J.R.
10. *T.B.L.*, pp. 163–4
11. Atwood, *op. cit.*, p. 268
12. J.R. Letter to author
13. *V.I.D.*, pp. 27, 45
14. Jean Rhys, *The Left Bank*, 1927, p. 85
15. *V.I.D.*, p. 62
16. *T.B.L.*, p. 162
17. 'T.P.', p. 71
18. *T.B.L.*, pp. 167–8
19. *Ibid.*, p. 41
20. J.R.; see also, 'The Bishop's Feast', *S.O.L.*, pp. 33–6
21. *V.I.D.*, p. 62
22. *Ibid.*, p. 28
23. Jean Rhys revisited Dominica in 1938

Two
The European

When the boat docked at Southampton, it was a grey, lowering English summer. The trees were drab, and the fields from the boat train seemed small and colourless. It was a desolate England only an emigrant from a hot, vibrant climate can know. Her aunt tried to cheer the desperately homesick girl. She showed Gwen St Paul's, Westminster Abbey, the Wallace Collection, Madame Tussaud's, zoos. And she was exasperated to find that her niece showed little interest.[1] 'I don't like London,' she was to have Anna Morgan say in *Voyage in the Dark* – Anna had also come from Dominica – 'It's an awful place; it looks horrible sometimes. I wish I'd never come over here at all.' 'You must be potty,' her friend retorted. 'Whoever heard of anybody who didn't like London?'[2]

But London with its noisy grey streets was a nightmare. The ruins of her grandfather's estate, her father's holiday house overlooking the sea, these were reality; although she was disturbed to find how quickly her memories began to fade. When she began school in Cambridge, her sense of desolation intensified. She stood in the cold class-room looking out of the window on a yellow-grey sky and thought desperately, 'What is going to become of me? Why am I here at all?'³ Then a girl she hardly remembered wrote from Switzerland praising her acting in the *Winter's Tale* as Autolycus. She had rolled off 'all those words . . . that Miss Born wanted to blue pencil' as if she had known what they meant, and 'made the other girls look like waxworks.'⁴ Perhaps at the back of Gwen's mind was also Nina in the Cuban circus, her age, the 'Only Girl Who Works Without a Net', weaving in the acetylene lamplight. Acting too was brilliant lights, costumes, the caught breath of drama. Not the arid routine of school. She wrote immediately to her father, asking to enrol in Tree's Academy (later to become the Royal Academy of Dramatic Art) in Gower Street, London. And her father agreed.

Installed in a boarding house in Upper Bedford Place, Gwen had made a decision that went against her family's advice. She was alone and inexperienced in a city unlike any place she had previously known. She had never been more in need of her father's support. But on the evening of 19 June 1910, he came home complaining of feeling tired, and was helped to bed. Within hours he was dead of a heart attack. Roseau and the surrounding villages, in particular those who were poor and black, made his funeral a demonstration of their affection. His coffin was placed in the open trap he had used for his visits, and it moved slowly through the choked streets to the English Cemetery, overlooking his beloved sea. Gwen was on vacation with relatives in Yorkshire when the cable came through with the news. At first she was calm. 'I didn't believe him.'⁵ Then the reality broke over her. She began crying and could not stop.

Continuing at Tree's Academy was now out of the question. There was no money, and the family had too many problems to keep an emigrée daughter studying drama. Gwen determined to take one of the few occupations that, at her age and status, would give her independence – she would go on the stage as a chorus girl. Her aunt was strongly disapproving; but the career had for the family the advantage of solving one of their many financial liabilities. She changed her name to Jean Rhys and went into vaudeville. She was to describe through one of her fictional heroines the offhand routine of being hired:

> Marya had longed to play a glittering part – she was nineteen then – against the sombre and wonderful background of London. She had visited a theatrical agent; she had sung – something –

anything – in a quavering voice, and the agent, a stout and weary gentleman, had run his eyes upwards and downwards and remarked in a hopeless voice: 'Well you're not Tetrazzini, are you, deary? Never mind, do a few steps.'

She had done a few steps. The stout gentleman had glanced at another gentleman standing behind the piano, who was, it seemed, Mr Albert Prance's manager. Both nodded slightly. A contract was produced. The thing was done.[6]

Once she was in the theatrical troupe, the glitter evaporated. The wages were barely enough for necessities, one pound fifteen a week, extra for matinees, but, if one were ill, 'no play, no pay'. This meant she had to use the dingiest rooms, and was constantly fighting the effects of hunger and cold. At nights she learnt how to put a blanket over the door with a bolster at the bottom to keep out the draughts, make a nest with any cushions or pillows on the floor, and huddle over the gas fire. But she was still cold. And she began to understand the 'pale, sad, mournful' expression glimpsed under Madame Rodriguez's greasepaint even touring in the tropics. Life in touring was 'an odd life. Morose landladies, boiled onion suppers. Bottles of gin in the dressing-room. Perpetual manicuring of one's nails in the Sunday train. Perpetual discussions about men. ('Swine, deary, swine.') Like Marya, Jean Rhys learnt 'to talk like a chorus girl, to dress like a chorus girl and to think like a chorus girl – up to a point. Beyond that point she remained apart, lonely, frightened of her loneliness, resenting it passionately.'[7]

She was not, she claimed, a good actress. She was too sensitive to forget herself and brazen out a part she could not believe in; she was liable to freeze and forget her lines in sudden stage fright. But she made a good figure in the chorus. She toured the north, all the streets like every other street, lowering with smoke, the theatre changing rooms cramped, infested with rats and cockroaches. On the stage the shallow scenery was painted with scenes of English country houses and rich interiors; the dialogue was such banalities as 'Going to Ascot? Well, if you don't get into the Royal Enclosure when you *are* there I'm no judge of character.'[8] And in the chasm of the pit terrifying rows and rows of north country faces. Life was hard, its austerity intensified by the fact that England was at war.

But here it is particularly important not to confuse fiction and real life. The fiction distils the pain into a poignant mood of desolation. The reality was more varied, tempestuous, robust. It had its boredom; also its heights and depths. Jean was passionate, dogged, and very pretty. She was not broken, she weathered the life, and even achieved a little success. She progressed to a company doing Vienna operas. She played a small part at the London Lyceum, doing *Cinderella* with Harry Champion and Gladys Roy. She was even signed up for an appearance in a film being made at Alexandra Palace. But she became bored and cold with the waiting about, changed out of her film costume, and went home.[9]

Music hall and concert trouping was a hard but formative period of Jean Rhys' life. She had to cope with loneliness, physical discomfort and illness, drawing on her own reserves. She learnt to observe others and herself, gaining insight into suffering, particularly of the isolated young woman, that was to form the basis for all her writing. Most important, she began to experiment with writing, not for publication, but as a way of coping with her own depressions, writing in exercise books the 'Diary' that was to go with her around Europe and was later to take shape as *Voyage in the Dark*.

Music hall itself was to help shape her particular art. She took over its juxtaposition of fantasy and tawdry reality; she used its motifs and rhythms to orchestrate her fiction. So the lonely Anna Morgan sings

> 'And drift, drift
>   Legions away from despair'

identifying not only with the song – which she cannot remember precisely – but with the plump girl she had heard singing it in Glasgow, whose contrasting pale-gold curls and long, stupid face reflect the poignancy of longing and dreariness she herself feels.[10] Tunes become the key to a mood, to meaning. In the short story 'Let Them Call it Jazz'[11] a song heard in prison becomes a private understanding of the state of the social outcast for the mulatto heroine. Indeed, there was a relationship between musical form and Jean Rhys' composition of prose.

In 1919, with the ending of the war, Jean's theatrical apprenticeship ended. She married the Dutch poet and translator Max Hamer, and left England for the Continent of Europe. If the

Caribbean was one mental world and England another, Europe was a third. Europe when the couple crossed the straits of Dover was in post-war turmoil. There were shortages and black markets, social upheavals as whole classes became poor and new elites came into power. In 1921 Max Hamer took a secretary's job with the Japanese legation in Vienna. The value of the Austrian crown was plummeting, and there was illegal trading and currency dealing, gold smuggling. The hotels and cafes were peacefully invaded by the armies of many nationalities, their legations and hangers-on – French, English, Italian, Japanese, American, Dutch, Belgian. 'Gone the "Aristokraten". They sat at home rather hungry, while their women did the washing.' [12] It could be a gay, mobile, hard world. Money was made and lost quickly. In the constant round of parties hearts were broken, or proved too hard to break, breaking others.

In the spring the city was glowing with white and mauve lilac. 'Always now I'll associate lilac with Vienna,' one of her heroines was to say, and with lilac 'the lights looking down from Kahlenberg, the old lady with the yellow wig singing of Frauen.' [13] Jean Rhys was to make Vienna the basis for an uncharacteristically romantic short story, 'Vienne', about a girl called Francine, who is in the city expecting a child. Her husband, however, is engaged in illicit currency dealings, and the couple alternate between excitement and despair as they dodge the police and poverty, finally fleeing across Europe in a fast car. [14] But Jean was likely to have seen more of the dull bourgeois side of Franz Josef's Vienna in the two years they were there. One excitement was the opera. The Japanese legation was given a box at the State Opera House, but after seeing a performance of *Madame Butterfly* – it was nothing like Japan, they assured Max – they gave the couple the box, to their continuing delight. [15]

Then on to Budapest, with its restaurants and ladies in white dresses. 'Budapest looks theatrically lovely from a distance,' Jean later wrote. 'I remember the moon like a white bird in the afternoon sky; the greyish-green trunks of sycamore trees . . . Then back to the city and its vivid smells, the wail of tzigane orchestras, the little dancer of the Orpheum.' [16] But it was Paris that became Jean Rhys' spiritual home. Paradoxically, it did not prove as alien as London. This was partly because Dominica, like the other islands that have a shared French and English history, had both French and English elements in its culture. Jean identified more strongly with the French side – Roman Catholic, cosmopolitan and with a greater acceptance of life – than with the more Puritan English tradition. Paris had grace and style. Far more than in England, Jean felt, women were respected. Paris was gay and cultured. She responded.

In the post-war period, Paris was the cultural centre of the world. Besides those settled there, such as Pablo Picasso and Jean Cocteau, writers and artists from both the Old and New Worlds came to Paris to discuss and to work. From the United States came Hemingway, Gertrude Stein, Fitzgerald, Djuna Barnes, the imagist poet 'H.D.', Ezra Pound, Hart Crane; from England, the Sitwells, Wyndham Lewis, and the naturalised Briton, Ford Madox Ford; from Ireland, James Joyce and Samuel Beckett. From the Black Caribbean came the Jamaican Claude MacKay. The list is not complete. Jean Rhys moved among the literary flames, seeing and meeting them, yet remaining largely untouched by their work. James Joyce she met, and found charmingly gentle; but she did not read him. Hemingway was genial to the shy English girl: she could not understand the tough image of him others seemed to have. She did not discuss her own ideas of fiction, if indeed she had formulated any. Her main extended piece of writing was in the exercise books, filled with spidery writing, she had kept from her chorus girl days when she would write to keep at bay her loneliness and depression. She showed them, not to a writer, but to Mrs George Adam, wife of the editor of the continental *Times*. Mrs Adam recognised them as intense and melodramatic, yet disturbingly convincing. She made some changes, and showed them to Ford Madox Ford, who immediately saw their author's incipient talent.[17]

Ford was in Paris from 1922, living with the Australian artist Stella Bowen. There he wrote three of his major novels, *Some Do Not . . .* (1924), *No More Parades* (1925) and *A Man Could Stand Up* (1926). He set himself up as a literary entrepreneur, and on Friday nights in 1924 he was giving literary parties in a small working-class dance hall called the Bal du Printemps in Montmartre. One reporter described the scene at one of these parties – 'and then, at another table much nearer the dancing floor, we see Stella and Olga and Jean and Ernest and Bill . . .'[18] Ernest was

Hemingway and Jean was Jean Rhys. One of Ford's literary ventures was *The Transatlantic Review* (1923–4), which attempted to be a focus for the creative work of the expatriate community. He published Hemingway and Gertrude Stein. He also claimed that he published 'as many as [he] could' of the sketches of Jean Rhys. The claim was ironic, or, more likely, intended to mislead: he published one piece, a brief sketch 'Vienne', which was to appear much extended in the collection of Jean Rhys short stories, prefaced by Ford, called *The Left Bank* (1927).[19] Under his aegis she worked on translations, including one of Francis Carco's *Perversité* (1928).

At the end of 1924 the *Review* collapsed, and Ford moved to a studio in the Rue Notre Dame des Champs, in Montmartre. There Jean lived with Ford and Stella. According to Stella, a hostile witness, she was at that time 'a really tragic person. She had written an unpublishably sordid novel of great sensitiveness and persuasiveness . . . [but] she had bad health, destitution, shattered nerves, an undesirable husband, lack of nationality, and a complete absence of any desire for independence. When we met her she possessed nothing but a cardboard suit-case and the astonishing manuscript.' Stella's account is as significant of the way Jean was regarded by the 'respectable' world as it is for Jean herself. 'She took the lid off the world that she knew, and showed us an underworld of darkness and disorder, where officialdom, the bourgeoisie and the police were the eternal enemies and the fugitive the only hero.' Jean made gallantry, taking risks, and sharing 'one's last crust' more attractive than 'patience or honesty or fortitude'. She taught Stella that 'You can't have self-respect without money. You can't even have the luxury of a personality.'[20] In Stella's rage, still simmering many years later, we hear the tones Jean Rhys was to reproduce in her fiction as the voice of respectability towards those reprehensible enough to be poor. 'I have set the machine in motion and crushed many like you. Many like you . . .'[21]

But Stella did not see Jean Rhys as a social threat alone. 'In order to keep his machinery running,' she wrote of Ford, 'he requires to exercise his sentimental talents from time to time upon a new object. It keeps him young. It refreshes his ego.'[22] The talented, vulnerable girl was such an object. He read her work and encouraged and guided her, helping her to avoid the falsely dramatic and to concentrate on the exploration of her own experience. His Preface to the collection of her sketches, *The Left Bank*, contrived to be both fulsome and patronising, but it was not imperceptive.

> I should like to call attention to her profound knowledge of the life of the Left Bank – of many of the Left Banks of the world . . . on the technical side . . . these sketches begin exactly where they should and end exactly when their job is done . . . Miss Rhys's work seems to me to be very good, so vivid, so extraordinarily distinguished by the rendering of passion, and so true, that I wish to be connected with it.[23]

Jean, naturally passionate, in these sketches prunes scenes and characters to the poignant essentials, and for this the experienced editorial hand of Ford takes some of the credit. His contribution to her life and the themes of her novels is ambivalent, but also important.

When Jean was finally sent off to the south of France to do some 'ghost' writing, her presence in Ford's household had created cracks in the relationship between him and Stella which were to break into open rupture three years later. The effect on Jean Rhys concerns us here only in its impact on her writing. Her first four novels all explore in different ways the experience of a girl being kept by a man who deserts her, and psychic search for an identity that follows that loss. Although Jean Rhys is not a self-consciously political writer, few novelists have made a more effective exposure of sexist exploitation. Few, if any, have revealed so vividly the way in which economic and social dependence can undermine a woman's psychic being.

Her first novel, *Postures* (1928, issued in America as *Quartet*, the title used by the Penguin reprint) may well, as Francis Wyndham suggests,[24] have startled Ford. It tells how Marya, an English girl in Paris left defenceless by the imprisonment of her husband, is taken into the predatory 'protection' of an Anglicised intellectual who resembled Ford down to his clumsy hands and hard blue eyes. His 'briskly broadminded wife', who cooperates in the affair, is very like the Stella who emerges from her autobiography. In the tragic ending, Marya loses both lover and husband. *After Leaving Mr Mackenzie* (1930) moves between Paris and London. Julia Martin has been abandoned by her lover, an Englishman in Paris; when his weekly cheque stops, she makes a desperate, doomed attempt to find a life for herself. *Voyage in the Dark* (1934) was written after her return to England brought on a flood of reminiscences for her earlier chorus girl life; it was based on the exercise-book 'diaries' she had written to keep depression at bay at that time. In *Good Morning Midnight* (1939) Sasha Jensen, over forty, revisits Paris; her fur coat, part of a front against the loss of her dignity, only attracts a gigolo thinking she is a rich woman looking for sex in return for money, and a tragi-comic relationship builds up towards a complex dénouement.

These novels brought Jean Rhys a modest reputation from the general reading public, and a deeper admiration from a few readers who recognised the extraordinary truth of her work. A typical review was that appearing in *The Times Literary Supplement* when *Good Morning Midnight* was published. The reviewer was suspicious of the sensitivity and self-awareness of the heroine – 'Sasha seems too often to confuse a fatal excess of temperament with the experience life has dealt her' – but was respectful of her honesty – 'time and again honesty comes to the rescue and enables Miss Rhys to escape sentimentality by the skin of her teeth.' The reviewer even thought that the handling of emotion 'goes a little in advance of, say, Mr Hemingway,' which was more of a compliment in 1939 than it might be today.[25] But, as Francis Wyndham has claimed,[26] her depiction of private emotion was ahead of its time.

In her ten years in Paris she had done a number of jobs – translating from her husband's manuscripts, tutoring a family in English, fashion modelling, and other work – besides her writing. Having divorced her husband, in 1934 she returned to England. Four years later, remarried to Mr Tilden-Smith, she revisited Dominica. The next year, she slipped out of public view, publishing nothing, and she was largely forgotten. In 1957 the B.B.C. Third Programme broadcast an adaptation of *Good Morning Midnight*, and the producer, Miss Vaz Diaz, traced her to her home in Devon. She was just beginning a new novel which Diana Athill of André Deutsch heard about and promptly commissioned. When this was published as *Wide Sargasso Sea* in 1966, winning the W. H. Smith Annual Literary Award for the best novel of the year, rediscovery of her work began. Her novels were republished by Penguin and her short stories collected by André Deutsch in *Tigers are Better Looking* (1968). Her story 'Temps Perdi' was chosen as one of the pieces to launch *Penguin Modern Stories* (1969). More recent stories and sketches have been collected in *Sleep it Off Lady* (1976). She is now receiving the fame and notice that in her early years was largely denied her. In 1974 A. Alvarez wrote, 'To my mind, she is, quite simply, the best living English novelist.'[27]

Fame has given her contacts and stimuli, but also brought many pressures. Against them she has preserved the self that lies also at the core of her artistic achievement. In a moving article on growing old, she wrote in *The Times*.

> If you've often tried in the past to put yourself to sleep by repeating 'nothing matters, nothing matters at all', it's a relief when few things really do matter any longer. This indifference or calm, whatever you like to call it, is like a cave at the back of the mind where you can retire and be alone and safe. The outside world is very far away. If you sometimes long for a fierce dog to guard your cave, that's only on bad days. Perhaps tomorrow will be a good day.[28]

Notes

1. J.R.; see also 'Overture and Beginners Please', *S.O.L.*, p. 71
2. *V.I.D.*, p. 40
3. *S.O.L.*, p. 70
4. *Ibid.*, p. 73
5. *Ibid.*, p. 75
6. *Q.*, pp. 14–15
7. *Ibid.*, p. 15
8. *T.B.L.*, p. 35
9. J.R.
10. *V.I.D.*, p. 90
11. *T.B.L.*, pp. 44–63
12. *Ibid.*, p. 195
13. *Ibid.*, pp. 195, 206
14. 'Vienne' first appeared in the *Transatlantic Review*, 6 December 1924, pp. 639–645; it was reissued, enlarged, in *T.B.L.*
15. J.R.
16. *T.B.L.*, p. 207

17. J.R.
18. Henry Gorman, 'Ford Madox Ford', *Bookman*, March, 1928, p. 57
19. See n. 14
20. Stella Bowen, *Drawn from Life*, 1941, pp. 166–7
21. *T.B.L.*, p. 81
22. Bowen, *op. cit.*, p. 165
23. *T.B.L.*, pp. 137–139
24. Francis Wyndham, 'Introduction', *W.S.S.*, p. 6
25. *T.L.S.*, 22 April 1939, p. 231
26. *W.S.S.*, p. 9
27. 'The Best Living English Novelist', *N.Y.T.B.R.*, 17 March 1974, pp. 6–7
28. *The Times*, 17 May 1975, p. 16; *My Day*, pp. 27–9

Three

The making of a writer

Mr Severn sat at his typewriter. 'By six o'clock the floor was covered with newspapers and crumpled, discarded starts of the articles which he wrote every week for an Australian newspaper.' The subject was there – the Jubilee of George V – , but the article would not come out. 'He couldn't get the swing of it. The swing's the thing – otherwise the cadence of the sentence . . . Words swirled round in his head, but he could not make them take shape.' So he went out, rushing down the stairs, had two double whiskeys, and began to lose himself in the night life of Wardour Street. He picked up two girls, the hard, brisk Heather and the plump, ageing and good-natured Maidie. The night progressed with a frenetic search for gaiety in a second-rate night club, and Mr Severn and Maidie finally got thrown out into the street, and spent the night in a police cell. The next morning Mr Severn suddenly realised he had what he had been searching for. The gaiety that was an escape from the sordid reality that remained thrusting beneath it – this was the mood of both his night out and the Jubilee celebrations. And the mood had its own style, its rhythm, which released Mr Severn to write about it. 'He had got it.' He sat down and, with great assurance, began typing.[1]

This story, which gives its title to Jean Rhys' volume of collected stories *Tigers are Better Looking*, is a significant statement about her art. Her writing is slow and laborious – *Wide Sargasso Sea* took nine years to complete – the painful writing and rearrangement of 'an almost incredible mass of tangled notes and drafts'[2] – to quote Diana Athill – out of which her fiction emerges. Yet her writing does not embody carefully constructed theories of art, and the critic is often hard pressed to analyse exactly where its extraordinary quality lies. Ford accurately called it a 'singular instinct for form.'[3] Each piece of writing has its own structure of mood and psychological meaning: Jean Rhys' genius is to write to a form and rhythm dictated by this structure. As Ford wrote, she *knows* exactly when to start and when to end.

This can be seen from the early pieces from *The Left Bank*, such as 'Hunger',[4] barely four pages, which simply orchestrates the effects of being without food. But even here we see her exploring incidents which, although themselves apparently simple, can bear the weight of much wider implications. In 'Mannequin',[5] for example, Jean Rhys sketches six hours in the life of a girl taking on a new job modelling in a fashion house, and makes it a paradigm of her initiation into a whole new way of life. Little actually happens. She takes on the job, models, eats, gets tired, is paid a compliment, leaves for the evening. Much of the complexity comes through the unobtrusive description of the fashion house. It is a world of reflections and contrasts – the front of the salons where the parades take place, bright and wonderfully decorated; while behind there is a desolate warren of corridors and staircases where Anna despairs of finding her way.

The fashion is sophisticated; the models are not persons, they are images. 'Coldly critical glances were bestowed upon Anna's reflection in the glass. None of them looked at Anna directly.'[6] It is a world of 'human flowers' whom she meets, each of which personified a distinct and separate type to which she had to keep, even in relaxation. Anna, ironically, images 'innocence'. By five Anna is exhausted but when at five she walks out down the Paris street with a new poise we realise that her initiation has been not only into fashion modelling but into the world of Paris for which the salon is one focus.

The 'machine' of society is a reality Jean Rhys was to explore through other images – such as the prison (in 'From a French Prison'),[7] a hospital ward (in 'Outside the Machine'),[8] or the 'respectable' family (in *After Leaving Mr Mackenzie*), – and the symbolism is all the more effective for being unobtrusive. The machine demands conformity of its members, or exacts a fearful toll. Some find a compromise. In a haunting sketch, 'Illusion',[9] Jean Rhys describes Miss Bruce, an English artist in Paris, prim but pleasant, tall, thin, 'a shining example of what character and training – British character and training – can do.' She remains 'sensible' amid the 'cult of beauty and the worship of physical love' that was Paris in the nineteen-thirties. She wears a neat serge dress in summer and a neat tweed costume in winter, and her only make-up is a little powder on her nose.

But when she goes suddenly to hospital with appendicitis the narrator, sent to fetch her night-clothes, is startled by the glimpse of a different identity. Miss Bruce's wardrobe is 'a glow of colour, a riot of soft silks.' Fine evening dresses, flame of old gold, a carnival costume, flowing crêpe de chine, all fill the rails. Then there is make-up of all kinds, and fine scents. Later, knowing that her secret has been discovered, Miss Bruce says, 'I should never make such a fool of myself as to wear them ... They ought to be worn, I suppose.' And her eyes wander in vicarious pleasure to a dark girl sitting nearby. '"Not bad hands and arms, that girl," said Miss Bruce in her gentlemanly manner.' 'Gentlemanly' perfectly associates a culture – English culture – and sexual repression, with hints of homosexuality. The sketch also implies the nature of art for Miss Bruce as a sublimation. But Jean Rhys, as narrator, is appalled by the obscenity of such waste. She imagines the dresses 'shrugging their silken shoulders, rustling, whispering about the *Anglaise* who had dared to buy them in order to condemn them to life in the dark ...'[11]

Others cannot or will not compromise with the machine. The poor – like the old man and the young boy who wait confused and wondering in the queue in 'From a French Prison',[12] contemptuously officiated over by the warders – are its victims. Particularly vulnerable in a society dominated by the wealthy, and where men hold the legal power, is the unsupported woman. It is she whom Jean Rhys was to explore with ever-deepening penetration through her fiction until, with Antoinette Cosway in *Wide Sargasso Sea*, a mad wife locked in an attic came to be the expression of the trauma of a whole historical era.

An outline of *Quartet*, her first novel, has already been given. Marya Hughes is a chorus girl who had joined Mr Prance's Number One touring company because she was 'a vagabond by nature', but soon found the dreary routine offered anything but freedom and adventure. She is rescued from this by a Pole, Stephan Zelli who lives by selling 'pictures and other things', a business conducted largely in cafés with objects changing hands in unobstrusive, shabby bags. The couple go to live in France. Stephan is a romantic, like Marya, but unlike Marya, he knows exactly where he is going. He is charming, gay, pets and makes expert love to Marya; but if Marya asks him anything he does not want to answer he becomes secretive and a liar. As Marya says, he is as 'natural as an animal',[13] and Jean Rhys never makes the mistake of equating animal or childhood 'nature', with innocence or goodness. As Aunt Cora says in *Wide Sargasso Sea*, 'unhappily children do hurt flies',[14] Marya lives a precarious but basically happy two years with him: then disaster strikes; he is sent to prison for theft.

The story is told by a third-party narrator, but already Jean Rhys is using the consciousness of the heroine as the autonymous centre of the work. If we see Stephan through Marya's eyes, we are aware of Marya through her own consciousness of the world around her. It modulates her surroundings: a glass of wine makes Paris 'significant, coherent and understandable';[15] news of Stephan's arrest sends the crowds 'cowering' beneath their umbrellas and the winter branches become 'ridiculously frail and naked arms', frail and naked to life as Marya feels herself.[16] The Heidlers are her natural predators. Where Marya's open nature leaves her totally vulnerable, the couple, 'fresh, sturdy people', briskly social, protect themselves by categorising, organising. '"H. J. and I have quite made up our minds that eating is the greatest pleasure in life. Well . . . at any rate, it's one of the few pleasures that never lets you down", says Lois.'[17] The choice of 'eating' is sinister. Not only does it indicate a basic lack of moral or spiritual values, but the Heidlers, for all their apparent energy, have an inner emptiness, a hunger that can only be satisfied by draining another human psyche. Heidler, although Jean Rhys does not call him this by name, is a vampire. Marya feels physically cold in his presence. Later she is to write to him, 'It's as if all the blood in my body is being drained, very slowly, all the time, all the blood in my heart.'[18] Lois, who helps provide Heidler with his victim, moralises, 'Victims are necessary so that the strong may ... become more strong.'[19]

Marya has few defences. When she first meets the couple, she notes the way Lois winces when Heidler speaks sharply, and thinks, 'I bet that man is a bit of a brute sometimes.' And 'as she thought it, she felt his hand lying heavily on her knee.' But her innocence betrays her natural instinct. It was 'ridiculous, not frightening. Why frightening?'[20] Heidler plays her into his grasp by exposing his inner weakness, 'Oh, God, I am so utterly sick of myself sometimes'; his wife plays on Marya's natural gratitude, 'I want to help you. I'll be awfully disappointed and hurt if you don't allow me to.'[21] Sexually besieged, Marya is outraged. 'Well, I kept off you, didn't I?' exclaims Heidler, 'I knew that I could have you by putting my hand out, and I kept off you. I thought it wouldn't be playing the game. But there comes a limit, you see.'[22] It is a favourite and significant phrase of Heidler's, 'playing the game'. But Marya cannot take life as a game. Moreover, desperately needing a father figure, she is caught in a web of love for Heidler only intensified by the moral confusion of the situation. Despised by outsiders as a 'kept woman', insecure in the growing awareness that Heidler is going to cast her off, and that her husband is coming out of gaol, she increasingly loses her self-respect. She humiliates herself with Heidler: 'I love you, I love you, I love you. Oh, please be nice to me'.[23] She retreats into herself. In the mirror she would 'stare at herself, feeling a horrible despair'.[24]

It is a central irony of the book that both Stephan and Marya have been psychically crippled by their experiences, and yet their traumas cannot bring them together; rather, they destroy each other through the weakness, insensitivity and lack of emotional control that suffering brings. Stephan is loving to Marya when he comes out of prison, but as a ghost might love: he slips off alone to Holland and then plans to go to Argentina, never responding to Marya's needs. Marya loves him, but resents him for what has happened to her. With the openness that made her vulnerable to Heidler, she also cannot help asserting her love for Heidler. When Stephan threatens to leave her, in desperation she tries to keep him by threatening to call the police, a menace that drives through to Stephan's most sensitive point, the private world of illicit dealings he would never allow Marya to discuss. He strikes her unconscious and leaves. In the one seriously false note of the book, we see Stephan picked up and being consoled by another woman by the time he gets out into the street.

'When you come out,' Stephan said of prison, '– but you don't come out. Nobody ever comes out.' [25] What happens the other side of spiritual death, loss of self-respect and the will to order one's life, becomes an increasing concern of Jean Rhys' fiction. In *After Leaving Mr Mackenzie* the break comes when the cheques sent weekly by Julia Martin's lawyer stop coming. 'Before that I'd always been pretty sure that things would turn out all right for me, but afterwards I didn't believe in myself any more.' [26] The loss of the money is not important, it is the betrayal of a relationship that forces the girl back on her own resources, only to find that her period of dependence had dried those resources up. At the heart of the book is a family drama. In her first book, Jean Rhys presented Marya as a woman broken by circumstance. Now she begins to explore backwards, searching for disease in the roots. Julia's mother is dying, longing for her one-time life in the warm vitality of South America. This brings the family together, but also exposes the rift between them and Julia. Julia had taken her independent line against a narrow and censorious family. Her sister Norah is the faithful daughter who had stayed to nurse her mother through a long illness: her resentment of Julia is intensified by a certain jealousy of her freedom. Julia, financially destitute and alone, resents her sister's security. In a scene where the aftermath of the death weakens both sisters' self-control, the hatreds and animosities come bubbling out, and Julia is thrust into the street by the indignant nurse. The scene is a heightened re-enactment of the family rejection that lay behind the betrayal of Mr Mackenzie, and we understand why his failure of trust now left her with nothing to turn to. But the power of the book is the psychological exploration of Julia herself – weak, self-destructive, craving affection yet incapable of making a loving relationship. Julia is a paradigm of the social outsider, presented twenty years before John Osborne wrote *Look Back in Anger*. 'If all good, respectable people had one face, I'd spit in it,' she screams at her sister. 'I wish they all had one face so that I could spit in it.'[27]

The family quarrel breaks her completely. Her expression becomes glazed. She makes only sporadic contact with reality. Climbing the steps of her house with a lover in the dark, the lover touches her and she breaks down screaming. She goes to Paris. In an ending, told with precise delicacy, she meets Mr Mackenzie, and, when he braces himself for a fierce assault, she only asks him for some money and another Pernod to drink.

The two novels that follow explore themes similar to the first. But there is a development in the technique. Both are first-person narratives, and progress by a delicate process of exploration and association, an interweaving of present and remembered past. As Sasha Jensen says in *Good Morning Midnight*, people's minds are not 'water-tight compartments . . . it's all washing about.'[28] Jean Rhys conveys this wash, this juxtaposition of ideas and reminiscences, while maintaining her sense of the pattern of mood and event. If an early influence on Jean Rhys's fiction is music hall, with its changes of mood and use of refrain, here the debt is to the montage and juxtaposition of film. Indeed, Sasha thinks of 'my film-mind' ('For God's sake watch out for your film mind').[29]

In *Good Morning Midnight* Sasha Jensen has been rescued from dying of drink and drugs in a Bloomsbury bed-sitter by a friend who sets her up with new clothes and enough money to get away from the depressing world of London. She goes to Paris, where she attempts to recover her old will to live. In these later works, the heroine has lost her passivity, and become a self-aware identity. Her psychological penetration, her evocation of states of depression and nervous breakdown, are even more extraordinary than in the later parts of *After Leaving Mr Mackenzie*. Panic can suddenly fall on her while eating alone in a restaurant. Some days she feels, inconsequentially, strong; on others the weakness returns. 'I must be very careful,' she tells herself, 'today I have left my armour at home.'[30] Her life becomes a routine of choosing between restaurants where she is liked and where she is disliked, friendly streets and hostile streets, rooms where she might be happy, rooms where she never could be. She puts on the armour of a new hair-style, a new hat. 'Please, please, monsieur et madame, mister, missis and miss, I am trying so hard to be like you. I know I don't succeed, but look how hard I try.'[31] But when two English girls happen to look at her in a restaurant and say 'Oh my God!', and others turn to look, she is naked, flayed, in extremity.[32]

The novel is in four parts, and on two time levels. 'This damned room,' she thinks at one point, 'it's saturated with the past. . . . It's all the rooms I've ever slept in, all the streets I've ever walked in.'[33] The humiliation of trying to find a room brings back memories of finding a job as a mannequin (one month that lasted), or a guide to Paris (one day only). Her depression after being insulted in a restaurant leads her to the depths of losing her child in a cheap Paris midwifery. 'There are people having babies all over the place. Anyhow, at least two are having babies.'[34] At first these memories appear to have no pattern. But, examined closely, one sees that they penetrate deeper and deeper through layers of her consciousness to the most significant moments of her life. They culminate, in the final section, in her remembrance of happiness with her one-time Dutch husband, the journalist Enno.

The memories here interweave with her being picked up by a gigolo who is after her money, and mistakes the coat assumed as 'armour' against the respectable world for a sign of wealth. He tells her a story of needing a passport to leave the country, which she does not believe; he does not believe that she has no money. She tells herself she can play his game because she has nothing to lose. 'He is out for money and I haven't got any. I am invulnerable.'[35] Yet, while she does not admit this to herself, she is drawn to him because he is in some ways like her husband of the past, Enno. Their love, too, emerged from cross-purposes and misdirected attempts to exploit. 'I haven't any money,' she thought of Enno, 'He hasn't any either. We both thought the other had money.'[36] However insincere, the gigolo has some human traits. 'He doesn't look like a gigolo,' Sasha thinks, ' – not my idea of a gigolo at all. For instance, his hair is rather untidy. But, nice hair.' He has suffered, with a scar on his throat from attempted suicide. Unscrupulous, even brutal, he is still a person.

Sasha surrenders herself to the game, becoming poised, even dominant. 'He throws back his head and laughs . . . "Very nice, very nice indeed. Beautiful teeth," I say in an insolent voice.' She begins to unwind, to rediscover something in herself that was wiped out long ago, even before meeting Enno, in childhood. 'I don't know what it is about this man that seems to me so natural, so gay – that makes me also feel natural and happy, just as if I were young – but really young. I've never been young.' [38] In the final scene the gigolo tries to make love to her. They are both a little drunk, it does not go well, and in despair she tells him to take some money and go. She has left herself totally vulnerable, for all the money she has is in the purse. He goes, leaving her bleeding and hurt, while she does not allow herself to look. But he has not taken her money. In her mind she brings him back to her, and when she opens her eyes, he is standing beside her. In its context, it is a profound statement about the nature of compassion. Through the novel Jean Rhys has stripped Sasha of all the meanings and associations of love, and left her hanging by the merest thread onto the will to live. Yet without denying any of this degradation she brings Sasha, miraculously, to a moment of love and meaning. It is the culmination of the search which has been passed through the four novels. It might be thought that it left its author with nothing further to say, for she published nothing more for some twenty years.

Yet when more writing did begin to appear, in the form of short stories, it showed Jean Rhys still developing. The four novels had moved successively deeper into the mind and sensibility of a central character. Now she combined the same vivid empathy with a masterful control of background scene and imagery that was the mature fruition of both her art and her experience. In 'Outside the Machine',[39] for instance, the character of the heroine is familiar. Inez is an outsider, an English girl in Paris without money thrust by appendicitis into the ward of an English hospital she cannot afford. She is alienated from her English home, and has wandered 'quite a bit' about Europe. The story is mediated through her consciousness, and Jean Rhys uses the drifting moods of the sick girl to explore different dimensions of the ward community. The 'aggressively respectable' Mrs Wilson is the cruel voice of the machine of English society. 'To which of the seven divisions, sixty-nine sub-divisions, and thousand and three sub-subdivisions do you belong?' [40] The gay chorus girl Pat is the alternate voice of vulgarity, placing a towel round her head and changing the ward into a stage by singing *The Sheik of Araby*, making the ward join in. Inez's spirit rises. 'There's lots of time before tomorrow,' she tells herself. Mrs Murphy, the neurasthenic whose attempted suicide evokes the hostile disgust of the ward and sisters (she has nice kiddies, and anyway, she's a woman, what right has she to do that?) echoes Inez's darkest depression. When the ward inmates wonder whether the attempt had been by Mrs. Murphy or Inez, she thinks *Well, it's both of us*.

Yet the strength of the story is that Inez's depressed consciousness is set off against the fully realised scene of the ward. It is a superb focus for the theme, fifteen beds in a tall narrow room cut off completely from the world outside: even the sky seen through the high placed windows has no colour. With economic precision, Jean Rhys establishes the impersonal routine which reduces the patients, with their individual crises, to pieces in a machine. When Inez finally makes a scene, swearing 'This and that to the lot of you!',[42] the nurse and doctor make no response, save a blink of the doctor's eye. It becomes clear that the title is ironical; the ward may be isolated from the world outside, yet it is a machine not only of routine, but a model of the machine of society, with its moral censors, its misfits and contrasting attitudes to reality. The extrovert chorus girl Pat is not only a foil to Inez but a character in her own right, turning even the ineffectual clergyman into a figure in her music-hall world – 'On and off like the Demon King – '[43]

Inez, sent out from the hospital before she is ready, partly, it is suggested, because she has not 'fitted in', faces a hopeless future with the peace that can come from despair. When a Mrs Tavernier, an English widow with two marriages behind her, one disastrous, identifies with her and gives her money, Inez is grateful but feels 'you can't die and come to life again for a few hundred francs'.[44] Yet the money is wrapped in a white linen handkerchief, trimmed with lace, and smelling of vanilla. She wears a gold ring, two roses, the petals touching each other. Unobtrusively, Inez's grief is set in perspective by the peace after suffering symbolised by the gold roses and the white linen.

Such relaxed, objective writing cannot be said to be finer than Jean Rhys' earlier work. From her first writing, almost all she has published has been validated by its authenticity, a truth not only of theme, but of theme expressed in the appropriate style. 'The swing's the thing', as Mr Severn declared, 'the cadence of the sentence.' Yet her work, apparently at first limited in its concerns, when examined, is shown to be a continual and self-denying quest for greater clarity, a more complex understanding. The quest was to culminate in *Wide Sargasso Sea*.

Notes

1. *T.B.L.*, pp. 64–77
2. Diana Athill, 'Jean Rhys and the writing of *Wide Sargasso Sea*', *Bookseller*, 20 August 1966, pp. 1378–1379
3. *T.B.L.*, p. 138
4. *Ibid.*, pp. 169–171
5. *Ibid.*, pp. 149–155
6. *Ibid.*, p. 150
7. *Ibid.*, pp. 145–148
8. *Ibid.*, pp. 78–100
9. *Ibid.*, pp. 151–155
10. *Ibid.*, p. 144
11. *Ibid.*, pp. 142–3
12. *Ibid.*, pp. 156–9
13. *Q.*, p. 48
14. *W.S.S.*, p. 30
15. *Q.*, p. 20
16. *Ibid.*, p. 22
17. *Ibid.*, p. 12
18. *Ibid.*, p. 121
19. *Ibid.*, p. 58
20. *Ibid.*, p. 13
21. *Ibid.*, p. 43
22. *Ibid.*, p. 57
23. *Ibid.*, p. 102
24. *Ibid.*, p. 97
25. *Ibid.*, p. 106
26. *A.L.M.*, pp. 37–8
27. *Ibid.*, p. 98
28. *G.M.M.*, p. 140
29. *Ibid.*, p. 147
30. *Ibid.*, p. 42
31. *Ibid.*, p. 88
32. *Ibid.*, p. 43
33. *Ibid.*, p. 91
34. *Ibid.*, p. 49
35. *Ibid.*, p. 64
36. *Ibid.*, p. 96
37. *Ibid.*, p. 65
38. *Ibid.*, p. 130
39. *T.B.L.*, pp. 78–100

40. *Ibid.*, p. 81
41. *Ibid.*, p. 97
42. *Ibid.*, p. 96
43. *Ibid.*, p. 86
44. *Ibid.*, p. 100

Four
The Caribbean in a cold place

The sensitive child never leaves home. The more contrasting the world into which the adult goes, the more the child is present, smelling the scents, tasting the foods, seeing the colours and forms of the years that shaped its sensibility. Jean Rhys left Dominica when she was sixteen, but nothing was to be as real, in her imagination or her art, as the long verandah of her father's holiday house, the garden ruins of old Genever, the colours and scents of Dominica. Even in her books written wholly about Europe, the sensibility is not wholly European. Her sensitivity to heat and cold, to bright colour or the absence of colour, her sense of another life behind the mask of society conventions, were formed in the Antilles.

The characters of her fiction, too, are rarely at rest in the physical present. The immediate exists as part of the remembered past, the past as part of the present. Her heroines are divided even from themselves, looking in mirrors repeatedly for an assurance or clue of identity, seeking a wholeness in love that is always betrayed. Jean Rhys expresses the archetypal conflict between the warm, sensuous tropics and the cold northern world. This by itself would be a cliché, a commonplace of both Caribbean and European literature and art. But in her work it is not a commonplace. What gives meaning to her distinction is that it is also that between the experience of childhood in the Caribbean – childhood with its innocence, acceptance, feeling – and adult responsibility in Europe, with the cruel compromise demanded by growing up. It is the meeting of four levels of experience. It is this that saves her portrayal of the Caribbean from false romanticism, giving it complexity and a wider significance.

Jean Rhys' most personal exploration of this theme is *Voyage in the Dark*. It is her favourite work, 'so true', she has called it.[1] Anna Morgan is a fifth-generation creole, with a Welsh doctor as father, cast adrift in England and living a monotonous life as a chorus girl in a third-rate touring company. She is Dominican – this is not mentioned directly but her island, 'all crumpled into hills and mountains as you would crumple a piece of paper in your hand' lies between 15° 10' and 15° 40' N. and 61° 14' and 61° 30' W.[2] which, as Jean Rhys would have learnt from her seafaring father, is the situation of Dominica.

The story is in four parts, moving with controlled momentum towards its tragic climax. In the first, longest section, Anna and her friend – Maudie, an extrovert foil to the sensitive main character – are picked up by two men at a seaside town. A relationship develops between Anna and one of the men. Walter Jeffries: at first it goes disastrously wrong, but she catches influenza, Walter looks after her, and tenderness grows. He sets her up in a decent room, and she arranges to take singing lessons instead of staying in the theatre troupe. But, by its nature, the liaison is doomed, although rejection shatters Anna. Then follows a short section in which Anna is foot-loose in London. She meets an old chorus-girl friend, Laurie, now a semi-prostitute, and has a disastrous night out with two pick-ups in a cheap hotel. Ethel, a 'masseuse', is setting up a dubious establishment for men in Bird Street, and thinking Anna's charms will be useful, persuades her to take a room with her as a 'manicurist', at the same time charging a steep rent. In the third section, Anna begins to form a relationship with Carl, an American; she discovers she is pregnant, and finally has to appeal to Walter for money for an abortion, an agonising and sordid operation in which the baby is killed within her so that it will be stillborn. In the final terrible climax she expels the dead child and the doctor says briskly, 'She'll be all right . . . Ready to start all over again in no time, I've no doubt.' [3]

The portrayal of the seedy London life is convincing, down to the details. Bird Street where Ethel 'practised' still exists behind Selfridges, and was an accurate location for such an establishment. It still has an air of uneasy respectability, although the area for 'massage' practices has changed, as has Ethel's décor of glazed chintz curtains, bowl of fruit, and stereotyped picture of 'The Cries of London'. The absurdity of the business erupts when Anna hears a crash and rushes in to find a blanketed man playing a hymn tune at the piano in embarrassment while his leg jerks up and down in involuntary agony. The couch had collapsed under the 'massage' and the man's foot had fallen into a bowl of water on the floor, which Anna had brought in too hot. In another scene Anna, out with Laurie and two men, tries to get a hotel room but the commissionaire, with a show of morality, insists they must have two rooms. Yet when Anna, drunk and sick, tries to hide herself in the second room, she discovers the double hypocrisy of the arrangement: it is a single bed, not meant for use – for there are no blankets – and no lock to the door. It is not only the observed detail that makes this fictionally effective, it is the way, as with the scenes with Ethel, that the detail reinforces the theme: the missing lock is not only an observation about the hotel, it intimates the vulnerability of Anna.

Character is portrayed with the same telling economy; even minor characters are individual and convincing. Ethel's brisk, calculating personality emerges from her rapid dialogue. She demands twenty-five pounds from Anna, but when Anna cannot pay this she comes down to eight. When Anna takes out two five-pound notes, puts back one, and changes it for three sovereigns – sensing, innocent as she is, that to ask for change would be perilous – Ethel flows on 'Of course, when I said I'd do it for eight quid I was making it as cheap as possible. God knows if I shall be able to manage. We'll have to see how things go . . .' [4] She appears brightly confident in her outrageous manipulation of Anna. Yet she collapses in jealous anger when Anna goes out and she herself is not invited; when Anna, dismissed, prepares to leave her, she threatens suicide. Her glib surface overlays her own loneliness and uncertainty.

Anna's adventures in London, however, are only one level of the book. The novel tells two stories, counterpointing each other until in the final section they tragically mesh. Anna, a withdrawn, reflective girl, exists in two worlds, that of the present and that of her Caribbean childhood. In the first words of the novel she tells us that on coming to England, 'It was as if a curtain had fallen, hiding everything I had ever known. It was almost like being born again. The colours were different, the smells different, the feeling things gave you right down inside yourself was different. Not just the difference between heat, cold; light, darkness; purple, grey. But a difference in the way I was frightened and the way I was happy.'[5] Sometimes she would shut her eyes and pretend that the warmth of the bedclothes or the fire was the sun; or imagine she was in the town of her childhood, 'looking down Market Street to the Bay'. 'Sometimes it was as if I were back there and as if England were a dream. At other times England was the real thing and out there was the dream, but I could never fit them together.'[6]

Jean Rhys not only tells us of the two worlds, she recreates them in Anna's consciousness so that we can understand the difference too. The luminous prose evokes the West Indian house with its verandah and latticed jalousies, dazed by the sun at noon, haunted by the moon at night. We see it throughout from the eye of the child, reacting with her responses to the wonder and fear of a moonlit boat-ride; or to the discomfort of Sunday, prickly in starched white drawers tight at the knees, white petticoat and embroidered dress, with brown kid gloves ordered from England and, by the time they arrived, one size too small – 'Oh, you naughty girl, you're trying to split those gloves; you're trying to split those gloves on purpose.' There is the misery of feeling the perspiration trickling under the arms and knowing there will be a wet patch in the armpit, 'a disgraceful thing to happen to a lady'. Then after the boredom of the service, a moment of release walking through the still palms in the churchyard. 'The light is gold and when you shut your eyes you see fire-colour.'[7] In the passages of memory the senses are all fully alive – sight, smell and touch.

And the sky close to the earth. Hard, blue and close to the earth. The mangotree was so big that all the garden was in its shadow and the ground under it always looked dark and damp. The stable-yard was by the side of the garden, white-paved and hot, smelling of horses and manure. And then next to the stables was a bathroom. And the bathroom too was always dark and damp. It had no windows, but the door used to be hooked a little bit open. The light was always dim, greenish. There were cobwebs on the roof. [8]

By contrast, descriptions of England are lacking in these qualities. The fields are 'squares like pocket-handkerchiefs; a small tidy look it had everywhere fenced off from everywhere else.' [9] The few sensuous details of England express alienation, 'the streets like smooth shut-in ravines and the dark houses frowning down'. [10] There is monotonous sameness. 'There was always a little grey street leading to the stage-door of the theatre and another little grey street where your lodgings were, and rows of little houses with chimneys like the funnels of dummy steamers and smoke the same colour as the sky.' [11] In the Caribbean, even a cobweb was a significant detail.

The lack of warmth and detail in the English landscape is echoed, for Anna, in the people. English people 'touch life with gloves on', Jean Rhys wrote elsewhere. [12] (Perhaps she was remembering Dr Nicholls.) There is little concern for other human beings, and in particular for women. 'Most Englishmen don't care a damn about women.' Values are focused on money and clothes. 'You can get a very nice girl for five pounds,' one man explains to Maudie, 'a very nice girl indeed; you can even get a very nice girl for nothing if you know how to go about it. But you can't get a very nice costume for her for five pounds. To say nothing of underclothes, shoes, etcetera and so on'. [13] The evaluation is that of an exploited, single girl in London. But extreme as it is, it is the reflection of a difference between life in a closely-knit island community and the impersonal materialistic life of an English city.

The division, however, was not only between Dominica and London; it existed in Dominica itself. The family circle, ruled over by Aunt Hester, caught in the straitjacket of being white and respectable, was a cold climate for the sensitive Anna. So Anna formed her deepest relationships with Francine, the black kitchen girl, a little older than herself, and so both mother and sister.

Francine is extrovert, laughing and singing. Anna listens to her songs and joins in the stories. 'At the start of the story she had to say "Timm, timm," and I had to answer "Bois sèche".' [14] When Anna has her first period, it is significantly Francine who tells her what is happening, and it all sounds natural; Hester then lectures her on it, making her feel soiled and ashamed. [15]

The white family resents Anna's friendship with blacks. 'Impossible to get you away from the servants. That awful sing-song voice you had! Exactly like a nigger you talked – and still do. Exactly like that dreadful girl Francine,' explodes Hester. [16] Anna is marooned between being white and being black. (In England, some friends call her a 'Hottentot', and she has fantasies of being of mixed blood as she remembers seeing the name of an illegitimate mulatto girl on a slave list, Maillotte Boyd.) [18] She loves Francine, but race dictates that Francine will hate her. She wants to be wedded to the sun, burnt black, or die. She goes deliberately under the midday sun without a hat and waits. 'The sun at home can be terrible, like God.' The sun punishes her for her presumption, and she is ill with sunstroke and then fever for some months. She turns, not black, but 'thin and ugly and yellow as a guinea'. [19] The simile identifies her with the European commercial world, in which she is stamped and coined irrevocably.

Through *Voyage in the Dark*, the two worlds interweave, the imaginary remembered world more real than the actual present. When Walter takes out the girl he has just met, he opens the door behind the dining room and it is a bedroom. She is shocked and frightened; he covers his awkwardness with forced casualness. She goes in shutting the door against him. The room, the bed, even the fire, are cold – 'The fire was like a painted fire; no warmth came from it.' [20] But she is drawn to Walter, and her flickering, incipient emotion is reflected in her observation of the brighter colours, the red of the lampshades. This evokes a sense of the Caribbean, and at the same time, significantly, of childhood. It had 'a secret feeling – quiet, like a place where you crouch down when you are playing hide and seek'. Love, when it comes, brings a web of warm memories. 'Thinking of the walls of the Old Estate House, still standing, with moss on them. That was the garden. One ruined room for roses, one for orchids, one for tree ferns.' And the sleep that follows is like the little death, sleep, taught in the Convent. 'Children, every night before you go to sleep you should lie straight down with your arms by your sides and your eyes shut and say: "One day I shall be dead. One day I shall lie like this with my eyes closed and I shall be dead."' Sex brings a flicker of Aunt Hester's condemnation of Maillotte Boyd, the illegitimate slave girl. *'But I like it like this,'* she thinks; *'I don't want it any other way but this.'* [21]

The childhood innocence she knew, both in Dominica and in her love for Walter, are betrayed, and the two levels run together in a startling image. Reading the letter in which she learns Walter is casting her off, she thinks suddenly of the verandah at home, creeping by her Uncle Bo, who is asleep, to pick up a magazine.

> I got up to the table where the magazine was and Uncle Bo moved and sighed and long yellow tusks like fangs came out of his mouth and protruded down to his chin – you don't scream when you are frightened because you can't and you don't move either because you can't – after a long time he sighed and opened his eyes and clicked his teeth back into place and said what on earth do you want child – it was the magazine I said – he turned over and went to sleep again. [22]

The image comes and goes. 'What's this letter got to do with false teeth?' she asks herself. But the relevance is complex. At one level the sudden transformation of her genial uncle into a sabre-toothed monster associates her betrayal by Walter with her rejection by the family, a rejection she may not fully realise as a child but which becomes clear in a heartless letter he writes to her Aunt Hester later refusing to help Anna. Deeper, it brings a terrifying crack in her whole sense of reality. Things are not what they seem. At another time, the image is reversed: an inanimate mask becomes alive. Uncle Bo's face becomes a hideous mask. But in the island masquerade Meta, Anna's black nurse, is wearing a huge white mask when, suddenly, she looks at the child and thrusts a contemptuous pink tongue out through the slit. Again, the child is terrified. [23] Both occasions are moments when the shock breaks out of a conflict of structures of reality, a trauma seen, in its widest sense, in Anna's confused cultural and racial identity. The shock splits her psyche at the roots. Her very personality is betrayed.

> I saw that all my life I had known that this was going to

happen, and that I'd been afraid for a long time, I'd been afraid for a long time. There's fear, of course, with everybody. But now it had grown, it had grown gigantic; it filled me and it filled the whole world. [24]

Towards the end she has a nightmare of sailing through doll-like islands in a glassy sea. One of the islands is her island, but the trees are wrong, they are English trees. Someone has fallen overboard. Drowning has appeared in the book as an image of abstraction and spiritual death. Thus when Walter had discarded her, 'It was like letting go and falling back into water and seeing yourself grinning up through the water, your face like a mask, and seeing the bubbles coming up as if you were trying to speak from under the water.' [25] When Anna returned to a party after hiding herself in a ladies' room her friend Laurie had told her, 'We thought you'd got drowned.' [26] But this time it is not Anna. Or is it? Is she dreaming of a scene of her own death? A sailor brings a coffin which opens and a child rises, a doll-like child-bishop. She wonders if she should kiss its ring. But it has a cruel face and eyes, and sways woodenly in the grasp of the sailor. Perhaps her child – her own childhood – is dead and condemns her. She tries to walk to the shore, thrusting through confused figures, but the deck heaves and she struggles helplessly. [27]

The images of falling, of violation, of drowning, of the mask, come together again in the terrifying climax of the book, the birth of her dead child. Physically, she experiences the giddy sensation of the world heaving and dropping away. The pains of sex, birth and death merge, and her protests against the fumbling midwife – 'stop, please stop' – mingle with remembered cries against violation by a white-faced lover. The fear, the remembered white face, recall another moment of terror experienced in childhood in Dominica, when she and her family were watching the masquerade of the black community through the jalousie slats. The dancer's masks are painted pink, with mocking blue eyes, straight noses and little heart-shaped red lips under which are slits for the dancer to thrust out his tongue. They are masks of mockery and hatred. Ironically, the white onlookers cannot see the satire directed against them – they see the dance only as proof of the blacks' lack of decency and self-respect.

You can't expect niggers to behave like white people all the time

Uncle Bo said it's asking too much of human nature – look at that fat old woman Hester said just look at her – oh yes she's having a go too Uncle Bo said they all have a go they don't mind.[28]

The remembered scene is punctuated by the cries of Anna – both as the terrified child and as the woman giving birth to her own stillborn baby – 'I'm giddy.' And the first-person 'I' of Anna the watcher changes to the 'we' of the dancers as she merges, in her imagination, with the dancers. '*We went on dancing forwards and backwards backwards and forwards whirling round and round.*' The surging pains intensify and now she is on a horse, swaying dizzily, with no stirrups to hold to, and the road leading along the sea and up through ghostly shadows to see '*a cold moon looking down on a place where nobody is a place full of stones where nobody is*'. She is falling but still she clings with her knees feeling very sick. She wakes. The dead child is born.[29]

The scene, like that of the nightmare with the doll-bishop, cannot be explained in terms other than itself. It brings together, with terrifying conviction, the actual agony of abortive childbirth and the levels of experience, the qualities of pain, that have emerged through the book, and lead them to the ultimate void, the wasteland in the cold moonlight. The ending echoes the beginning: both describe childhood impressions of Dominica. Her past is her future fate, waiting like a trap to destroy her. But the lonely ruin is not only a profound image of her own desolation. The image reminds us of T. S. Eliot's *The Waste Land*; like Eliot's desert, it is the expression of a spiritual state and the symbol of a culture laid waste by its history.

In this decayed hole among the mountains
In the faint moonlight, the grass is singing
Over the tumbled graves, about the chapel
There is the empty chapel, only the wind's home.[30]

The haunted, ruined plantation house had appeared earlier in the story, a memory associated with a moment of love, planted with flowers. Anna's tragedy leads her intuitively back in time before even her birth, before the ruins were made into gardens. She is led into the collective consciousness of her history, its historical and psychological roots. But for a fuller exploration of this intuition, we must examine *Wide Sargasso Sea*.

Before this, however, it is rewarding to look at a complementary short story that appeared in *The London Magazine* for 1962, 'Let Them Call it Jazz.' It is Jean Rhys' one story written throughout in dialect. It is life seen from the other side of the racial barrier. Selma Davis is a mulatto girl born on Martinique of a white father and mulatto mother, and brought up by her black grandmother. She emigrates to England, and ends up in Notting Hill. In England, she is estranged and friendless. Her attitudes to time, to money, to joy itself, are alien to England. 'I don't trouble about money,' she says, and is an easy prey for her Notting Hill landlady who robs her of all her savings, then throws her out because she has no money. She is picked up by a Mr Smith, a shady property developer who likes to keep a woman as an unpaid housekeeper in the buildings he buys speculatively. She has a quickened sensibility towards colour and light. In the decaying house, her eye picks out the few flowers in the garden. She describes the weather with estranged eyes, 'not much rain all the summer, but not much sunshine either. More of a glare.'[33] She spends what money she has on gas for heating, and on a little wine to lighten her spirits: drinking it, her depression lifts and she can sing.

But tensions build up with her 'nice' neighbours. '"Must you stay?",' they ask in a very sweet quiet voice, '"Can't you go?"' Selma uses her song as a defensive weapon against this genteel thuggery. As she retreats into the street, and her courage builds up, she sings louder, and the police arrive, suspiciously quickly. Cautioned, she gets drunk; she takes her shoes off and dances in the street. The scandalised 'nice' neighbours protest. 'Now young woman, take yourself off' . . . 'At least the other tarts that crook installed were *white* girls.'[34] She throws a stone through the hideous stained glass windows of her persecutors, and ends up in prison.

The shock, accompanied by illness and hospitalisation, is her spiritual death. She, like Anna, is trapped in the trauma of race and history. 'As for me I never will try again. It all dry up and hard in me now. That, and a lot besides . . . There's a small looking glass in my cell and I see myself and I'm like somebody else. Like some strange new person.' Characteristically, her personality had expressed itself through song. In the tenement, surrounded by hostile neighbours, she sang her grandmother's proud songs:

> Don't trouble me now
> You without honour
> Don't walk in my footstep
> You without shame [35]

She tried to make up her own songs, without much success. She does not have the right song for the strange land. When she is in prison she thinks 'I'm here because I wanted to sing.' Song is the expression of her personality, of her individual freedom. But song is communal too. Suddenly she hears a song, a song that the prisoners have made the expression of their free wills within the goal. 'It's a smoky kind of voice, and a bit rough sometimes, as if those old dark walls theyselves are complaining, because they see too much misery – too much. But it don't fall down and die in the courtyard; seems to me it could jump the gates of the jail easy and travel far, and nobody could stop it.' [36] Hearing it, Selma must have felt as slaves felt hearing a negro spiritual in another time and place.

Selma leaves prison. She has a succession of jobs, ending up dressmaking for a London store. At one party she whistles the prison song. It is heard and used by a composer, who makes it into a hit tune. At first she feels desolate, as if the most private of her possessions has been taken from her. But then she knows that it can never be taken from her: the music of suffering and defiance is never destroyed. The story is a remarkable imaginative feat. In it Jean Rhys takes on the other mask, the mask of a black Francine, also marooned in a divided world, and intimates that the suffering that divides can also reveal the universality of human experience.

Notes

1. J.R.
2. *V.I.D.*, p. 15
3. *Ibid.*, p. 159
4. *Ibid.*, p. 114
5. *Ibid.*, p. 7
6. *Ibid.*, pp. 7–8
7. *Ibid.*, pp. 36–8
8. *Ibid.*, pp. 36–7
9. *Ibid.*, p. 15
10. *Ibid.*, p. 16
11. *Ibid.*, p. 8
12. *Q.*, p. 9
13. *V.I.D.*, p. 40
14. *Ibid.*, p. 61
15. *Ibid.*, p. 59
16. *Ibid.*, p. 56
17. *Ibid.*, p. 12
18. *Ibid.*, p. 48
19. *Ibid.*, p. 63
20. *Ibid.*, p. 21
21. *Ibid.*, p. 48
22. *Ibid.*, p. 79
23. *Ibid.*, p. 151; see also L. Honeychurch, *The Dominica Story*, 1975, pp. 94–5
24. *V.I.D.*, p. 82
25. *Ibid.*, p. 84
26. *Ibid.*, p. 103
27. *Ibid.*, p. 140
28. *Ibid.*, p. 157
29. *Ibid.*, p. 158
30. T. S. Eliot, 'The Waste Land', in *Collected Poems 1909–1935*, 1936, p. 76
31. *T.B.L.*, pp. 44–63
32. *Ibid.*, p. 47
33. *Ibid.*
34. *Ibid.*, p. 54
35. *Ibid.*, p. 55
36. *Ibid.*, p. 60

Five

Wide Sargasso Sea

Ripples spread outwards from a flung stone. The pebble is Dominican history; the ripples move towards the imaginative vision of *Wide Sargasso Sea*. In 1824 John Potter Lockhart of Old Jewry, London – Jean Rhys' greatgrandfather – acquired the 'several plantations and estates in Dominica . . . now known by the name of Genever Plantation', some 1213 acres and 258 souls.[1] Three other partners in the venture dropped out of the story. The road today – past Loubière and over Morne Eloi – is tarred, if narrow, winding, and made dangerous by passenger and produce lorries plying between Roseau and the settlements of Grand Bay. But the journey the Lockharts made must have been much like that described by Jean Rhys a century later.

> The road goes along by the sea. The coconut palms lean crookedly down to the water . . . You turn to the left and the sea is at your back, and the road goes zigzig upwards. The feeling of the hills comes to you – cool and hot at the same time. Everything is green, everywhere things are growing. There is never one moment of stillness – always something buzzing. And

then dark cliffs and ravines and the smell of rotten leaves and damp . . . There's a bird called a Mountain Whistler, that calls out on one note, very high-up and sweet and piercing. You ford little rivers. The noise the horse's hoofs make when he picks them up and puts them down in the water. When you see the sea again it's far below you. [2]

There, clustered above Grand Bay was the plantation house, with its broad verandah, and then the little wooden slave huts, the coffee fields struggling against the encroaching bush, and, beyond, the great presence of the island.

The Lockharts came at a time of upheaval and change. But upheaval had been continuing since the island was first settled. Dominica was fought over by the French, who held neighbouring Martinique and Guadeloupe; by the British, who governed Antigua, St Kitts and Barbados, and the Caribs, who made Dominica one of their last retreats, fighting both the English and the French. In 1763 Britain took over the island, and attempted to overbear its predominant French character by encouraging massive settlement from England. They introduced sugar, which prospered, and for a few years Roseau became a prosperous international port. But in 1778 Dominica again became a cockpit for the two warring nations. It was recaptured by the French, who harassed the English settlers, and when the British retook the island in 1783, the French encouraged the runaway slave forces. These emerged from their mountain retreats to murder, steal and burn. A house guard was formed, and a series of raids were made on these settlements, until in 1814 the Maroon leader Jacko was taken, and over five hundred of his settlement captured or killed. In one of these attempts, General le Grange briefly occupied and burnt Roseau, leaving with a large ransom extorted from the inhabitants. When peace came in 1815, the island economy was severely shaken, and Anglo-French settler relations deeply hurt.

The treaty of Amiens promised renewed prosperity. But, as Jean Rhys was to write, 'you are getting along fine, and then a hurricane comes, or a disease of the crops that nobody can cure, and there you are – more West Indian ruins and labour lost. It has been going on for more than three hundred years'. [3] In 1829 coffee blight began the destruction of the coffee industry, and on 1 August 1833, the liberation of the slaves undermined the organisation of the sugar plantations. The ending of slavery did not resolve the hatreds of slave history. The Lockharts on their plantation were isolated and vulnerable. At first they attempted to surround themselves with Europe. The inventory of their Great House includes paintings and prints, music books, two pianos, 'one Jewel Case containing two Coral Necklaces, one Garnet do., Rings, Brooches, Ear-rings and other ornaments, Wine and Liqueur Glasses, one Inlaid Rosewood Dressing Case'. [4]

But on 2 October 1837, James Lockhart died, leaving his widow, who continued to run the estate through her overseer. In 1844 there was a census on the island. Rumours spread that it was the preliminary to a return to slavery. The black population rioted. At Genever, on Jane Maxwell's deposition, 'the estate was broken into by a body of the labouring people and every article therein . . . either stolen or destroyed'. [5] The house was burned down, and Jane barely escaped with her life. It was a night the like of which Jean Rhys was to recreate in *Wide Sargasso Sea* – the leaping red flames in the dark, the menacing black faces, the screams of the horses, and, beyond the flames, the great tropical night and the mountains. The house was never rebuilt. When another was made, the old ruins became a garden, 'one ruined room for roses, one for orchids, one for tree ferns. And the honeysuckle all along the steep flight of steps that led down the room where the overseer kept his books'. [6] Then in 1932 the blacks burnt down the new house.

The young Gwen Williams visited the plantation and was fascinated by its story. But the ripples spread still wider. In the dining room in Roseau, Gwen had seen a print of a Carib, the islanders Columbus met as Dominica's first inhabitants. She read about them in a closely-printed book with gaudy pictures. They still inhabited the Salybia reservation, with their smooth black hair, their slanting eyes, high cheekbones and copper skins. They never inter-married with the black population. Their women had a language secret from the men, it was said, going back to the days when they killed the Arawak men and took the Arawak women as wives. When Jean Rhys went back to the island in 1938, she went to see them. The remaining Caribs were sad but dignified. Their little houses were neat, surrounded by little flower gardens, the walls inside covered with 'pictures cut from newspapers and coloured cards of Virgins, saints and angels'. [8]

But the Caribs themselves were not like the print in the family dining room. The crippled girl who posed for a photograph had long brown creole eyes and hair that 'went through every shade from dark brown to copper and back again'. [9] Her mother had a Chinese look. The Caribs themselves reflected the many races that had settled in the Caribbean, and, behind them the Arawaks who were massacred by the Caribs and Spanish. The spectrum of races included Jean Rhys herself. 'Now I am home,' she felt, lying in the reserve under her mosquito net, 'where the earth is sometimes red and sometimes black. Round about here it is ochre – a Carib skin'. [10] In the Atlantic, currents carried vegetation from the shores of the world to meet in a great net of weed that could trap ships and men. Like the Caribbean islands. Like the wide Sargasso Sea. In a real bed of history an imaginary heroine waited to be born.

This heroine was to emerge from the dark corners of Charlotte Brontë's *Jane Eyre* (1847). Looking back to Jean Rhys' childhood, one can understand why the book should appeal to her. As Kathleen Tillotson has written of the book's first appearance, 'the profounder explorations of *Jane Eyre* were new indeed to the novel; not before in fiction had such continuous shafts of light penetrated the "unlit gulf of the self" – that solitary self hitherto the preserve of the poets'. [11] The inwardness, the poetry, surrounding not a Gothic heroine, but the childhood and working career of an ordinary girl, would find a pertinent echo in Gwen's own nature. Jane narrated:

> No; moonlight was still, and this stirred; while I gazed, it glided up to the ceiling and quivered over my head . . . My heart beat thick, my head grew hot; a sound filled my ears, which I deemed the rushing of wings; something seemed near me; I was oppressed, suffocated: endurance broke down; I rushed to the door and shook the lock in desperate effort [12]

Lying in the moonlight, terrified by Meta's stories of jumbies and vampires, Gwen knew Jane's childhood terrors herself. Isolated from her family, save for her father, she would have responded to Jane's loneliness at Gateshead and Lowood.

Jean Rhys' novel has so often been taken as a rehandling of Charlotte Brontë's story that it is important, at the outset, also to stress the contrast between *Jane Eyre* and *Wide Sargasso Sea*. The latter work is different in essence both from any fictional model and indeed from Jean Rhys' earlier work. For the great effect of the literary link was that of a release. Both the strength and the limitation of Jean Rhys' previous work is its fidelity to experience. She writes fiction, but her imagination meticulously explores what she knows; she rarely moves away from themes based on memory. Here, however, the literary starting point set her free to explore experience imaginatively in a new and more open way. From the first clipped sentences – 'They said when trouble comes close ranks, and so the white people did' – the story works at an intense emotional voltage. Everything serves to hold this power – the terse prose rhythms, the spectrum of brilliant sense impressions, the narrative flow itself, which becomes increasingly jagged and elliptical, leaping from vivid episode to vivid episode, but leaving shadowy gaps which tantalise and haunt the reader's imagination. It is difficult to relate this to West Indian life without appearing to subscribe to tourist clichés about the exotic Caribbean. Yet the point must be made. Purified, vivid and cruel in the heat of Jean Rhys' imagination, the essence of the book is the intensity of one aspect of the Caribbean experience. And this is intimately served by the style and texture of the novel as a whole.

Jane Eyre moves to a more leisurely tempo. It also embodies Charlotte Brontë's particular compromise with her temperament and with the Victorian period. She and her sisters had watched their brother, Branwell, destroy himself with imagined wrongs, and with alcohol. Her hero, Rochester, when he meets Jane Eyre, is heir to an illegitimate child, an insane wife, and self-tormenting passion. 'Bitter and base associations have become the sole food of young memory: you wander here and there, seeking rest in exile: happiness in pleasure – I mean in heartless, sensual pleasure – such as dulls intellect and blights feeling.' [13] Before he can be redeemed for marriage, he must have self-discipline; he must desire good and lose it. His physical maiming and blindness, and the death of the fearful wife in the attic is his purgation from his past.

Jane, too, must be strong enough to renounce her love for Rochester before proving worthy of receiving it. Jane's self conquest is convincing. The question hangs over Rochester. Not only is there an unresolved conflict between the heroic, tormented figure Jane sees, and the egocentric, hollow figure that his description and speech can make him appear to be; but the plot may be said to cheat. The love between Rochester and the independent Jane can only be consummated when illness changes him from the dominating figure Jane has loved. His moral weaknesses are focused symbolically in the insane wife in the attic, and finally burnt. But what is the implied cost to human values in the burning? What about the wife in the attic?

Bertha Rochester, as Charlotte Brontë portrays her, is a hideous incarnation of Rochester's uncontrolled self, of brute animal passion:

> In the deep shade, at the farther end of the room, a figure ran backwards and forwards. What it was, whether beast or human being, one could not, at first sight tell: it grovelled, seemingly, on all fours; it snatched and growled like some strange wild animal: but it was covered with clothing, and a quantity of dark, grizzled hair, wild as a mane, hid its head and face . . . the clothed hyena rose up, and stood tall on its hind-feet . . . The maniac bellowed: she parted her shaggy locks from her visage, and gazed wildly at her visitors. I recognized well that purple face – those bloated features. [14]

Readers of *Jane Eyre* will remember Rochester's story. His father had been 'an avaricious, grasping man'. He sent Rochester, at twenty-six, to marry the daughter of a planter and merchant for her dowry of thirty thousand pounds. On the other side the planter, Mr Mason, wants to acquire for the family good English stock: 'her family wished to secure me because I was of a good race; and so did she'. He found Bertha 'tall, dark . . . majestic', and flattering. After the marriage the thunderbolt falls. Her mother is a confined lunatic, her younger brother, a dumb idiot. She herself has an animal nature, 'her cast of mind common, low, narrow, and singularly incapable of being led to anything higher, expanded to anything larger . . .' She degenerates quickly into unmentioned vices and violence. 'Bertha Mason, the true daughter of an infamous mother, dragged me through all the hideous and degrading agonies which must attend a man bound to a wife at once intemperate and unchaste.' [15] Brought back to England confined as a lunatic, she attempts to burn Rochester in his bed, attacks her brother Richard

Mason with a knife, and finally burns Thornfield Hall down before her estranged husband.

Unless one is prepared, it is possible to read *Wide Sargasso Sea* until near the end without realising any link with *Jane Eyre*. Clues are given – the name Mason, although Jean Rhys alters *Jane Eyre* to make him Antoinette's step-father; the name Antoinette which Charlotte Brontë gives as one of Mrs Rochester's ('Antoinetta'); [16] the marriage in Spanish Town Jamaica. But these are coincidental details, the name Rochester is not mentioned, and it is only in the final sections, with the imprisonment in the attic under the care of Grace Poole that the unprepared reader would come finally to see the links. The books has its independent life, the other side of a mirror of social and racial consciousness. Its setting is precise: the breakup of the old Caribbean plantation society, and the marooning of the creole whites who had neither money nor blackness to secure themselves an identity.

It begins, as was required by Charlotte Brontë's story, in and around Spanish Town, Jamaica. Jean Rhys had never been to Jamaica, and her account of the lush vegetation of Coulibri, with its mossy stones and deep pools, is more characteristic of Dominica than of the dryer, lower Jamaica, a thousand miles away west north-west. It is only in the second part of the book that it moves to the honeymoon island in the outer Antilles. The two-island setting, however, is more than a nod towards *Jane Eyre*. The honeymoon island is associated with the unfallen world of nature – until Rochester enters it – of Antoinette's childhood memories. It holds a greater beauty and height – 'What an extreme green', muses Rochester as he looks up to the hills. [17]

Importantly, Jean Rhys also uses the two islands to point a contrast between cultures that cuts across race. Both French and English planter societies shared general moral degeneracy. Yet the quality of life they shared is very different. The French culture was characteristically Roman Catholic, more liberal, tolerant and refined. French slaves were encouraged to take Mass, and the elite were later educated to become black Frenchmen. If the equal terms they were offered were French terms, there was also a greater human acceptance, in particular after the French Revolution, which had a complex and profound effect on the black communities of the Caribbean. The English tended to be Protestant, more racially exclusive, and more materialistic. Antoinette, her mother, her nurse Christophine,[18] and even her playmate Tia – the daughter of the non-Jamaican Maillotte – are an island of French culture and all that it signified in the English-orientated Jamaica. 'You don't like, or even recognise, the good in them,' Antoinette's mother tells Mr Mason, speaking about the blacks, 'and you won't believe in the other side.'[19]

Alone in Coulibri, Antoinette enjoyed a profound, indeed pantheistic, relationship with the landscape. She was sure 'everything was alive . . . everything'. The place 'was sacred to the sun,' she says –   but it is not the benevolent Pantheism of Wordsworth. Her world is bounded with menace, even of nature. '. . . I was always happy in the morning, not always in the afternoon and never after sunset, for after sunset the house was haunted, some places are.'[20] When asked by Rochester if she believes in God she says it does not matter because 'we can do nothing about it, we are like these'. And she flicks from the table a moth that has been drawn inevitably into the flame of the candle and killed.[21] The island is like the Garden of Eden, but after Adam's fall had estranged mankind.

> Our garden was large and beautiful as that garden in the Bible – the tree of life grew there. But it had gone wild. The paths were overgrown and a smell of dead flowers mixed with the fresh living smell. Underneath the tree ferns, tall as forest tree ferns, the light was green. Orchids flourished out of reach or for some reason not to be touched. One was snaky looking, another like an octopus with long thin brown tentacles bare of leaves hanging from a twisted root. Twice a year the octopus orchid flowered – then not an inch of tentacle showed. It was a bell-shaped mass of white, mauve, deep purples, wonderful to see. The scent was very sweet and strong. I never went near it.[22]

Yet in a world of human menace, the indifferent natural universe is solace. After being chased by a black girl singing 'Go away, white cockroach, go away, go away . . . Nobody want you', she sits close to the old wall at the end of the garden. 'It was covered with green moss soft as velvet and I never wanted to move again.'[23] There she is safe.

Man's fall is both metaphysical and social. Immediately after her

account of her Coulibri garden, she refers to the effects of slavery
being abolished: 'All Coulibri Estate had gone wild like the garden,
gone to bush. No more slavery – why should *anybody* work?' [24] And
it is the social disorder that evokes active menace from the natural
and the supernatural world. It is after Mr Mason has come to
Coulibri and is imposing European (English) order on the past that
Antoinette has her first intimation of evil in Christophine's *obeah*.

> Yet one day when I was waiting there I was suddenly very
> much afraid. The door was open to the sunlight, someone was
> whistling near the stables, but I was afraid. I was certain that
> hidden in the room (behind the old black press?) there was a
> dead man's dried hand, white chicken feathers, a cock with its
> throat cut, dying slowly, slowly. Drop by drop the blood was
> falling into a red basin and I imagined I could hear it. No one had
> ever spoken to me about obeah – but I knew what I would find if I
> dared to look. [25]

'No one had ever spoken . . . but I knew.' The sentence is important.
Up to this point she was a natural part of her world; now her vision
is becoming divided. She becomes conscious of what was too close
for her to be aware of, and knows it as hostile. We are prepared for
the terrifying climax of the book when she attempts to use the
forbidden *obeah* to bring back Rochester's love.

In the divided world there is the potential for reconciliation. One
possibility is offered by Tia, the black girl from Martinique who is
Antoinette's one childhood friend, and with whom she identifies.
The other is offered by her mulatto cousin, Sandi. We know very
little about Sandi and his relations with Antoinette. We meet him
first protecting Antoinette from the albino boy and black girl who
close in on her as she is going to school. [26] Later she meets him
'often' when Rochester is away or while out riding, and Daniel
intimates sexual intimacy. [27] Whether this existed or not does not
matter: the tragedy is that race and social constraints have
prevented the natural relationship between Antoinette and the tall,
genteel mulatto from culminating in marriage. Social pressures
also undermine Antoinette's friendship with Tia. When she comes
home in Tia's dress, Tia having stolen hers, Antoinette's mother
'saw I was growing up like a white nigger and she was ashamed of
me,' and 'it was after that day that everything changed'. [28] The

scandalised mother orders Tia's dress to be burned, and with Christophine works in a frenzy to make a new one, perhaps selling her last ring to buy the material. On Tia's side, the relationship is destroyed by jealousy and greed. Antoinette has been given some pennies by Christophine. They shine 'like gold in the sun' – they are beautiful. Tia cheats her of them and then steals her dress.[29]

The hatred that robs Antoinette of her dress burns down Coulibri Great House. Mr Mason, who is devoid of love, can have no knowledge of hate. As the mob violence increases, his language retreats into rhetoric. 'They will repent in the morning. I foresee gifts of tamarinds in syrup and ginger sweets tomorrow.'[30] The burning is described with an extraordinary combination of swift narrative and evocative detail. The reader is placed in the centre of the turmoil, people running, rolling smoke, the finding of the dead, burnt Pierre by a mother shocked into madness; then flight, the precarious escape. Yet the account is remembered in terms of sensuous detail, the smells of the mother's burnt hair, the vanilla scent on Aunt Corah's shoulder, the black pool of water over which the smoke rolls relentlessly, the light of the sparks and flames. The fire becomes an incandescent centre to the book, from which neither Antoinette nor her mother can escape, and to which Antoinette is to be drawn at the end as a moth to a terrible candle flame. The link between the burning of Coulibri and that of Thornfield Hall is emphasised by the falling parrot, in flames, whose death stills the rioters into superstitious silence and saves their victims. The parrot, like Antoinette, has been trapped by its owner: Mr Mason had clipped its wings, as Rochester is to imprison Antoinette, and in each case the result is fatal. The incident shows the superstition of the blacks, but it is more than this. The parrot is taken as an image of the soul;[31] it is through their religious sense that they are shocked into a fear of killing. To kill a parrot is unlucky, if killing a white man is not.

While the house is burning, Antoinette sees her friend Tia and runs to her. 'As I ran, I thought, I will live with Tia and I will be like her. Not to leave Coulibri. Not to go. Not.' She does not see the jagged stone Tia throws into her face, nor feel the pain. The two are held in a dream-like moment of paradoxical unity and division. 'We stared at each other, blood on my face, tears on hers. It was as if I saw myself. Like in a looking-glass.'[32] Afterwards she suffers a long illness, and her hair is cut off. She hopes it will grow darker, like Tia's. She asks her aunt to sing, not an English song, but a negro spiritual, 'Before I was set free,' 'free' bearing all the tragic ambiguity of release and isolation.[33] She is told her wound will not spoil her for her wedding day. But, as she tells Rochester, 'I think it did spoil me for my wedding day and all the other days and nights.'[34] The divided mirror she glimpsed looking at the weeping Tia could never be mended.

But before Antoinette faces the final stages of her tragedy, Jean Rhys provides an interlude of peace. Its significance is highlighted by the scene that leads on to it, where Antoinette is pursued down the road by two menacing figures, a black girl and an albino boy expressing all the terror of an unnatural union of black and white: 'he had a white skin, a dull ugly white covered with freckles, his mouth was a negro's mouth and he had small eyes, like bits of green glass. He had the eyes of a dead fish. Worst, most horrible of all, his hair was crinkled, a negro's hair, but bright red, and his eyebrows and eyelashes were red.'[35] She escapes from the terror through the doors of her Convent school. It is a charmed garden, freed from all conflict. Even the saints are not images of struggle, but of fulfilment. 'The saints we hear about were all very beautiful and wealthy. All were loved by rich and handsome young men.'[36] Racial differences exist in the Convent, but do not matter; there are no mirrors allowed, there is no seeking for identity. When her stepfather comes to take her away he says 'You can't be hidden away all your life,' and she wonders, 'Why not?'[37] But she cannot escape. When Tia had stolen her dress she had a nightmare of being alone in the forest, followed by someone who hated her. Now the dream returns and expands. She goes from the forest into an enclosed garden following someone whose face is black, not by race, but with his hatred. The trees are strange. She follows up steep steps, where she clings to a tree that sways and jerks. '"Here, in here," a strange voice said, and the tree stopped swaying and jerking.' The nightmare ends in hiatus, preparing us for the nightmare of reality to come. The trees are English trees.[38]

In Part Two, the point of vision switches abruptly to that of Rochester, and his ascent up the mountain to the honeymoon house immediately associates him with Antoinette's nightmare. It is important, however, not to dismiss him simply as a villain. 'If you imagine that when you serve this gentleman you are serving the devil,' says Rochester's housekeeper to Grace Poole, her future keeper, 'you never made a greater mistake in your life. I knew him as a boy. I knew him as a young man. He was gentle, generous, brave.' [39] When we first see him, he is recovering from nearly three weeks of fever – 'I am not myself yet.' He is weak and debilitated. 'Everything is too much, I felt as I rode wearily after her. Too much blue, too much purple, too much green. The flowers too red, the mountains too high, the hills too near.' [40] It is a convincing gloss on Charlotte Brontë's account of Rochester's experience of the West Indies, oppressive except when 'a wind fresh from Europe blew over the ocean and rushed through the open casement: the storm broke, streamed, thundered, blazed, and the air grew clear'.[41]

We also see other, less acceptable sides to him. He is very much concerned with what society thinks of him. When Antoinette, with a sharp intuition, tries to call the marriage off, his one thought is the figure he will cut. 'I thought that this would indeed make a fool of me.' He does not make either a generous gesture of renunciation or a firm demand that she go through with the ceremony. He makes a wooden speech, saying, 'I will go with a sad heart'.[42] It is difficult to define this as either sincere or insincere. Like Mr Mason speaking of 'gifts of tamarinds in syrup and ginger sweets tomorrow' in the middle of a murderous riot, Rochester does not have the vitality to make real contact with reality: he retreats into rhetoric which distances him from his situation, avoiding the responsibility of humane action. By contrast Antoinette is immediately warm, physical, compassionate; although perhaps her action shows more intuition than she is aware of. '"Your sad *heart*," she said, and touched my *face*.' [43] Connected with his desire for respectability, he is also deeply concerned with race. As he begins to recover from his fever, he looks at Antoinette with growing suspicion. Is she racially pure? 'Long, sad, dark alien eyes. Creole of pure English descent she may be, but they are not English or European either.' [44]

Yet the tragedy to come is heightened by the possibility of the alternative. Here we see the genius Jean Rhys in setting the second half of the story not in Jamaica but in Antoinette's home island. Behind the multiple crisis of the Cosways – white against black, the decay of the plantocracy, French perspectives against English – lies the serene height of Granbois. The green is more intense, the flower scents more overwhelming. 'Cloves I could smell and cinnamon,' recounts Rochester, 'roses and orange blossom. And an intoxicating freshness as if all this had never been breathed before.'[45] It is the Garden of Eden of Coulibri, but before the fall of man. Both he and Antoinette are transformed. '"This is the boundary of Granbois." She smiled at me. It was the first time I had seen her smile simply and naturally. Or perhaps it was the first time I had felt simple and natural with her.'[46] Antoinette becomes gay and poised. She will put a crown of frangipani on his head and be a queen to his king. '"This is my place",' she tells him, '"and everything is on our side."'[47]

The switch from 'my' to 'our' is tragically ironic. But disaster is in the future. In a house empty of all but himself and Antoinette, Rochester drinks the toast, 'to happiness'. Watching her asleep he curses his failure to see her goodness when he nearly allowed her 'to escape'.[48] ('Escape' is again ironic and menacing.) He wishes to learn the secret of the place: 'It was a beautiful place – wild, untouched, above all untouched, with an alien, disturbing, secret loveliness. And it kept its secret. I'd find myself thinking, "What I see is nothing – I want what it *hides* – that is not nothing."'[49] Nor is he only a passive receiver. He becomes sexually potent, initiating Antoinette into sexual love, and their love is passion without guilt, as in unfallen Eden. 'Here I can do as I like,' they tell each other.[50] Significantly, sections of the book here alternate the voices of Antoinette and Rochester without a break: both consciousnesses become as one.

Their innocent love brings them into the abyss of the unconscious, with its dark conflict of passions; 'Desire, Hatred, Life, Death came very close in the darkness.'[51] But destruction does not come from this, it emerges from the trauma of history. A letter comes from one calling himself Daniel Cosway claiming that Rochester was betrayed into marriage with a congenitally unstable woman with a mad mother and an idiot brother. Rochester's self-image of respectability and 'good race' are threatened. Daniel, with his thin yellow face, is the voice of Caribbean history. His name is that of an Old Testament Prophet and he speaks with Biblical tones facing a text framed on a dirty white wall, 'Vengeance is Mine'. Behind him, a heavy black and gilt clock tolls the time. As he speaks, the accumulated hatred of generations of slave culture spill out,

distorted by envy and pride. Old Cosway's memorial tablet says
nothing 'about the people he buy and sell like cattle. "Merciful to
the weak", they write up. Mercy! The man have a heart like stone.'
He, Daniel, was a victim, Antoinette's half-brother, casually begot
and forgotten by Cosway.[52] We never know if this is true,
Christophine vehemently denies it.[53] Perhaps Daniel himself does
not know. But whatever the historical truth, Daniel's accusations
are lies against the realities of hope and love. As Antoinette says
wearily, the old days 'are forgotten, except the lies. Lies are never
forgotten, they go on and they grow'.[54]

Rochester at first rejects Daniel in anger. But his suggestions,
like Iago's to Othello, germinate. The parallel with the Shakespear-
ean play is relevant: while Othello is more noble, both he and
Rochester live in gestures and ideals, defenceless where a little
humane common sense would have saved them. Futher, there is
more than a little of Daniel in Rochester. Both are mercenary:
'What is five hundred pounds to you?' asks Daniel, 'to me it's my
life';[55] Rochester married Antoinette for money, 'The thirty
thousand pounds have been paid to me without question or
condition.'[56] Both are obsessed with racial purity and miscegen-
ation; both have an inflexible Puritan morality. Rochester turns on
Antoinette with tones that remind one of Daniel – '"And you," I
said. "Do you believe in God?"'[57]

Antoinette fights desperately to keep Rochester. She is passionately in love. '"And then,"' Christophine is to tell him, '"you
make love to her till she drunk with it, no rum could make her
drunk like that, till she can't do without it."'[58] It is love that seems
incommensurate with the object, but Jean Rhys knows, and had
recorded in Marya's love for Heidler in *Quartet*, that sexual love
does not depend on goodness or attractiveness of personality.
Antoinette, like almost all Jean Rhys' heroines, is in need of a father
figure, and Rochester's very paternal inaccessibility draws her like a
moth to a flame. For him she draws out all that is most intimate and
precious to her – place, flowers, candlelight, sun – unaware that
each influence makes the weak Rochester feel more insecure, more
determined to reject her. Finally she turns to the deepest
intimations of the 'black' side of her identity, the power of *obeah*.
Her journey to Christophine's cottage, like Rochester's to the
honeymoon house, is upwards, too high. Looking at a dark green

mango tree she thought, ' "what a beautiful tree, but it is too high up here for mangoes and it may never bear fruit," and I thought of lying alone in my bed with the soft silk cotton mattress and fine sheets, listening.' [59]

Christophine, with a wise understanding of both Antoinette and Rochester, tells Antoinette to leave her husband, at least for a while. This Antoinette cannot do. She is prevented not only by her love for Rochester, but, ironically, by her 'English' personality. While half her childhood has been dominated by the desire to be black (like Tia), the other half is formed by the associations of a 'white' home. This side is imaged in the picture of 'The Miller's Daughter', an idyllic figure pink and placid, which remains in her mind as her idea of her English self.[60] She wants to go to England. 'I will be a different person when I live in England and different things will happen to me.' [61] She wonders if she could borrow money to go alone; she does not stay with Rochester in order to go to England; but England is part of Rochester's appeal, part of the self she cannot understand but nevertheless longs for. Against all Christophine's advice – Antoinette the white (*béké*) girl should not meddle in black modes she cannot understand – Antoinette gives Rochester a love potion. Rochester makes violent love to her. Rochester never tells us this – he does not have the language to describe it, or perhaps even the psychic resources to experience it consciously – he awakes from it as from a nightmare of being 'buried alive',[62] an image of being plunged into his subconscious. The forces released are those of lust, which a cerebral personality like Rochester cannot control. He makes love to the black Amélie, knowing that Antoinette can listen, tortured, on the other side of the thin partition. This turns the story of Rochester in *Jane Eyre* on its head. There he tells of the unspeakable depravity of Bertha after the marriage. Jean Rhys shows the sexual and moral degeneracy as Rochester's.

Antoinette is not the only one lost. Rochester also has become the victim of Antoinette's love. In *Jane Eyre* Bertha is described as 'the foul German spectre, the Vampyre',[63] and later acts as one, literally fastening her teeth on Mason and sucking his blood. In *Wide Sargasso Sea* Antoinette's eyes become like a *soucoyant* (vampire), she becomes 'drunk' with Rochester's love, until 'she can't do without it'.[64] She sucks his precarious identity with her

passion and the powers of the island place. 'I feel that this place is
my enemy and on your side', he tells her.[65] Like Othello when his
love for Desdemona is gone, Rochester loses his bearings and his
feelings are in turmoil. 'It's an English summer now, so cool, so
grey. Yet I think of my revenge and hurricanes. Words rush
through my head (deeds too). Words. Pity is one of them. It gives
me no rest.'[66] The civilised arts of poetry and music become
distasteful. Again like Othello, having doubted one woman, he is
plunged into a bedlam of imagined lusts. The whole world is fouled.
'Do you think that I don't know?' he asks, 'She thirsts for *anyone*,
not for me.'[67] The only way out, both for Othello and for Rochester,
is death, either physical or psychic. Rochester does not kill
Antoinette's body, but he suffocates her soul. 'She'll not laugh in the
sun again . . . Made for loving? Yes, but she'll have no lover, for I
don't want her and she'll see no other.'[68] He does not knife himself,
but he swears never again to love. ' . . . If I was bound for hell let it
be hell. No more false heavens.'[69] He knows he cannot escape the
consequences of love and his rejection. 'She had left me thirsty and
all my life would be thirst and longing for what I had lost before I
had found it.'[70]

Rochester kills Antoinette by destroying both her identity of
place and her identity of soul. 'I loved this place and you made it into
a place I hate,' she tells him; 'I used to think that if everything else
went out of my life I would still have this.'[71] Now she has nothing.
Even before the abortive attempt with the love potion, he has
begun to undermine her sense of self. When she pours out her past
to him, inviting understanding, he calls her not Antoinette, but the
heavy Saxon name Bertha. 'Not Bertha tonight', she pleads; 'Of
course, on this of all nights you must be Bertha', insists Rochester.[72]
Antoinette is practising one form of *obeah*; Rochester counters
with another. 'You are trying to make me into someone else, calling
me by another name', says Antoinette, 'I know, that's obeah too.'[73]
As she heard her new name, 'I saw Antoinette drifting out of the
window with her scents, her pretty clothes and her looking-glass.'[74]
She becomes not even Bertha, but 'Antoinette, Marionnette', a doll,
his doll. A vampire himself, he drains her life. 'My hate is colder,
stronger (than yours),' he says, 'and you'll have no hate to warm
yourself. You will have nothing.' He makes her his puppet. 'No, the
doll's smile came back,' he says as they were leaving the house, ' –

nailed to her face.'[75]

Rochester and Antoinette are destroyed both by weaknesses within themselves, and by circumstance. Their ruin is part of a cycle in West Indian history. Antoinette's disastrous marriage is a repeat of her mother's with Mr Mason. However close the couple come to fulfilment, the treacherous voice of Daniel Cosway is waiting with the lies of Caribbean history. As Rochester receives Daniel's letter he feels no surprise. 'It was as if I'd expected it, been waiting for it.'[76] After his nightmare experience of the love potion he sits on the bed for Amélie, 'for I knew that Amélie would come'.[77] When the couple first arrive at the honeymoon house a moth blunders into the candle and lies stunned. 'I hope that gay gentleman will be safe,' says Rochester.[78] But the 'gay gentleman' is Rochester, and he is doomed as surely as the moth in the flame. Later, Antoinette flicks a dead moth off the table as she tells him 'It doesn't matter . . . what I believe or you believe, because we can do nothing about it.'[79]

England is the inevitable climax of the tragedy. England, as Christophine warned, appears unreal to Antoinette. It is a 'cardboard' world. This does not mean that a 'real' England does not exist. At one rare moment Antoinette glimpses this: 'There was grass and olive-green water and tall trees looking into the water. This, I thought, is England.'[80] But as Rochester feels the secret of Granbois is hidden from him, the true England cannot be experienced by Antoinette. So she retreats, in the 'cardboard' house, into her own inner world. Daniel's room was ruled by a materialistic clock; Thornfield Hall, too, is ruled by a clock, made symbolically of gold ('Gold is the idol they worship.').[81] But Antoinette's world moves to image and colour. 'Time has no meaning,' she thinks. 'But something you can touch and hold, like my red dress, that has a meaning.'[82] Like the section given to the idiot Benjy in Faulkner's *The Sound and the Fury*, the final part of the book is the brilliant evocation of the consciousness of a disordered mind. Yet this consciousness has more *truth* than the cardboard world of Rochester's normality.

The ending[83] brings together the images 'reality' has confused through the book. We remember Christophine's protective presence; the grandfather clock and Aunt Corah's patchwork; the garden and the 'tree of life'; the moss on the garden wall against which she huddled from the world; the doll's house, the picture of the Miller's Daughter; the parrot who shrieked out against the stranger *'Qui est là?'* – 'Who is there?' – and the nightmare of the man, his face black with hate; Tia standing by the pool. The dominant image is red and flame, the symbol of passion, both love and hate, of kind sun and cruel fire. The images and recollections associate into a meaning, into a logic that lies both within and outside Antoinette herself. 'Now at last I know why I was brought here and what I have to do.'[84] She goes out of her prison carrying a candle to burn down Thornfield Hall and herself falls from the burning building as she had seen the parrot fall whose wings had been clipped by Mr Mason.

The ending can be seen as an inevitable tragedy, the repeated cycle of violence that had in effect killed her mother with the burning of Coulibri – as she insists to Rochester, 'She did die when I was a child. There are always two deaths, the real one and the one people know about.'[85] We are reminded of the plantation house of Jean Rhys' own grandparents, burnt down not once but again and again. Hatred and lies have no ending. Passion has been pitted against cold reason, and passion has been destroyed.

Yet there is an opposite perspective. Rochester had determined to kill Antoinette more thoroughly than by a knife. 'My hate is colder, stronger,' he tells her, 'and you'll have no hate to warm yourself. You will have nothing.' He sees the life die in her eyes and triumphs – 'She was only a ghost, a ghost in the grey daylight. Nothing left but hopelessness.'[86] But Rochester does not destroy her. He does not even reduce her to the pitiful depraved creature we see in Antoinette's mad mother. In England, she preserves her passion, and a world of sensations and images that reflect her knowledge of reality. At the end, she asserts the values of heat and light against the darkness. Jean Rhys does not show us her death. We are left with the image of her carrying the flickering light down a dark corridor that cannot overcome it.

Notes

1. The negotiations began in 1813, when Lockhart was evidently at least visiting the island. They continued until the agreement found its final form in 1837. See Dominica National Archives, High Street, Roseau, folios Q.4. 136; D5. 522–600; Q.4. 136–9; Q.4. 66; H.5. 65–100.

2. *V.I.D.*, p. 129

3. 'T.P.' p. 81

4. Dominica, *Minutes Hon. House of Assembly*, 2 July 1844, pp. 22–3

5. *Ibid.*

6. *V.I.D.*, p. 45

7. S. A. W. Boyd, *Historical Sketch of Grand Bay*, Roseau, 1976, pp. [113]12—12

8. 'T.P.' pp. 82–88

9. *Ibid.*, p. 87

10. *Ibid.*, p. 139

11. K. Tillotson, *Novels of the Eighteen-forties*, 1954, pp. 260–1

12. Charlotte Brontë, *Jane Eyre* (1847), ch. 2, Penguin ed., p. 49

13. *Ibid.*, ch. 20, p. 247

14. *Ibid.*, ch. 26, p. 321

15. *Ibid.*, ch. 27, pp. 332–334

16. *Ibid.*, ch. 26, p. 318, cf. *W.S.S.*, p. 127

17. *W.S.S.*, p. 58

18. 'Christophine' is the name of a vegetable in the Antilles; it would appear to be unusual as a girl's name. Like Antoinette and Tia, she comes to Jamaica as a stranger.

19. *W.S.S.*, p. 28

20. *Ibid.*, p. 109

21. *Ibid.*, p. 105

22. *Ibid.*, pp. 16–17

23. *Ibid.*, p. 20

24. *Ibid.*, p. 17

25. *Ibid.*, p. 26–7

26. *Ibid.*, pp. 41–2

27. *Ibid.*, p. 103

28. *Ibid.*, p. 109

29. *Ibid.*, pp. 20–21

30. *Ibid.*, pp. 32–3

31. Compare with Wilson Harris' use of the parrot as the symbol of the human spirit in *Palace of the Peacock* (1960), 'I tell you when you pelt she (his parrot) you pelt me,' 115; I have not located the tradition in obeah, which does not mean it does not exist there. The bird has been

an archetypal image of the spirit in many mythologies; it appears in
this way in Coleridge's *The Rime of the Ancient Mariner*.

32. *W.S.S.*, p. 38
33. *Ibid.*, p. 40
34. *Ibid.*, p. 39
35. *Ibid.*, p. 41
36. *Ibid.*, p. 45
37. *Ibid.*, p. 49
38. *Ibid.*, p. 50
39. *Ibid.*, p. 145
40. *Ibid.*, p. 49
41. *Jane Eyre*, Penguin, pp. 335-6
42. *W.S.S.*, p. 66
43. *Ibid.*
44. *Ibid.*, p. 56
45. *Ibid.*, p. 61
46. *Ibid.*, p. 59
47. *Ibid.*, p. 62
48. *Ibid.*, pp. 61-2, 76
49. *Ibid.*, p. 73
50. *Ibid.*, p. 77
51. *Ibid.*, p. 79
52. *Ibid.*, pp. 100-104
53. *Ibid.*, p. 132
54. *Ibid.*, p. 108
55. *Ibid.*, p. 104
56. *Ibid.*, pp. 59, 102
57. *Ibid.*, p. 105
58. *Ibid.*, p. 126
59. *Ibid.*, p. 90
60. *Ibid.*, pp. 30, 155
61. *Ibid.*, p. 92
62. *Ibid.*, p. 113
63. *Jane Eyre*, Penguin, pp. 311, 321
64. *W.S.S.*, p. 126
65. *Ibid.*, p. 107
66. *Ibid.*, p. 135
67. *Ibid.*
68. *Ibid.*, p. 136
69. *Ibid.*, p. 140
70. *Ibid.*, p. 141
71. *Ibid.*, p. 121
72. *Ibid.*, p. 112

73. *Ibid.*, p. 121
74. *Ibid.*, p. 147
75. *Ibid.*, pp. 140–1
76. *Ibid.*, p. 82
77. *Ibid.*, p. 115
78. *Ibid.*, p. 68
79. *Ibid.*, p. 105
80. *Ibid.*, p. 150
81. *Ibid.*, p. 154
82. *Ibid.*, p. 151. Jean Rhys wrote that she 'lost belief in herself' on coming
     to England at the precise moment when she was forced to chose a drab
     dress instead of a 'pretty wine-coloured one.' ('Overture and
     Beginners Please', *S.O.L.*, p. 17)
83. *W.S.S.*, pp. 154–6
84. *Ibid.*, pp. 155–6
85. *Ibid.*, p. 106
86. *Ibid.*, pp. 140–1

Wide Sargasso Sea
and the Caribbean novel: an afterword

It may appear perverse to relate *Wide Sargasso Sea* to West Indian, or European, literature. It exists in its own right as a work of imaginative power. Yet as the poetry of Yeats gains a particular dimension when seen in the perspective of Irish literature, or Melville in the American, so consideration of the Caribbean qualities of Jean Rhys masterpiece can give particular insights. It does, indeed, give especial pleasure to those who are intimate with the West Indies. It is no paradox that the novel written furthest from a Caribbean childhood should be most densely informed with this world: memory can intensify experience. The speech rhythms of the different racial groups – whether Creole, mulatto or Afro-Caribbean – are unobtrusively distinguished, and right. The social and racial relationships are accurate.[1] The sensuous data of colour, scent and atmosphere are heightened but redolent of the Antilles. And the imaginative texture of the book perfectly matches the exploration of facets of Caribbean history.

The first critic to claim the novel's Caribbean qualities was the Trinidadian Wally Look Lai.[2] These lay not in the Caribbean setting, he declared, but in the way in which this setting was used.

The novel was different in kind from those Jean Rhys had written earlier. Previously she had explored the predicament of individual heroines: in *Wide Sargasso Sea* the personal theme becomes symbolic of a whole historical process.

> The West Indian setting, far from being incidental, is central to the novel: it is not that it provides a mere background to the theme of rejected womanhood, but rather that the theme of rejected womanhood is utilised symbolically in order to make an artistic statement about West Indian society, and about an aspect of West Indian experience.[3]

Antoinette's predicament, for Look Lai, is symbolic of the psychic experience of the white West Indian Creole denied a place in the old plantation world, or the new Caribbean society. Her 'madness' is not clinical insanity, but the logical expression of a fragmented consciousness. Its success lies not in any presentation of historical evidence, but in the poetic power with which the dimensions of history and the imagination fuse. The final passage is a superb culmination of all that has come before. She dreams of Tia. When she chooses to leap from the battlements, writes Look Lai, the choice is a positive one, 'to save herself from an existence which [has] become a form of death'. She seeks release not in the alien coldness of England, but in 'a return – however difficult – to the spiritual world on the other side of the Wide Sargasso Sea'.[4]

Later critics have in the Caribbean have followed Look Lai's emphasis on the novel's West Indian theme. Kenneth Ramchand, in *The West Indian Novel and its Background* (1970),[5] places *Wide Sargasso Sea* in a group of novels that also explore the trauma of the racially white Creoles in the evolving Caribbean. These include Phyllis Shand Allfrey's *The Orchid House* (1955) and Geoffrey Drayton's *Christopher* (1959). He relates them to Frantz Fanon's analysis of decolonialisation in *The Wretched of the Earth*. Fanon describes the white minorities facing a 'terrifying future' in the liberated ex-colonies, without status or power in the face of the hostility of the majority. The white Creole novel likewise express a 'terrified consciousness' which defines their theme and style.[6] Dr Ramchand's approach here has its limitations: a white Creole novel such as *Christopher*, for instance, is as much concerned with problems of adjustment to destructive parents as to the historical situation. On the other hand, it does place Jean Rhys' novel in an area of Caribbean writing, and Dr Ramchand's list of white Creole novels could be increased, notably with Edgar Mittelholzer's emotionally violent 'Kaywana' trilogy about the white plantocracy in Guyana.[7]

A different approach was taken by the Jamaican novelist John Hearne. Hearne saw *Wide Sargasso Sea* as centrally West Indian in its regard for 'the precious and irreplaceable *person*', in its concern with the human, and with the quest for love – albeit love doomed by its very intensity to failure. It is this concern that Europe, in Rochester, cannot understand. Nor does the dimension of Europe exist in the book only in Rochester. It appears in the very inception of the novel itself, for it was a European classic that brought Jean Rhys' work into existence. This he sees as a 'superb and audacious metaphor of so much of West Indian life'. He asks; 'Are we not still, in so many of our responses, creatures of books and inventions fashioned by others who used us as mere producers, as figments of their imagination; and who regarded the territory as a ground over which the inadmissible or forgotten forces of the psyche could run free for a while before being written off or suppressed?'[8]

Two Danish scholars, Hanne Neilsen and Flemming Brahms, have on the other hand seen the book's Caribbean significance as lying not in its counterpoint to Europe, but in its qualities of universal myth.[9] Their complex interpretation is based on the more recent thought of the novelist Wilson Harris.[10] For Harris, the layers of cultural inheritance in the Caribbean are not the grounds for conflict and alienation; they lie dormant waiting be reactivated, and to emerge transformed in the cultural possibilities of the present. Nielsen and Brahms show the book indicating three main 'strata' – the Creole, the Afro-Caribbean, and the *nouveaux riches* newcomers, such as Mason and Rochester.

In order for Coulibri to progress from its tragic past, its inhabitants have to break though the prisons of their old identities. One failure in this is seen in the breakdown of the relationship between Antoinette and Tia. Another comes when Rochester fails to rise to the union with Antoinette and all she offers: instead he withdraws into himself. This betrayal appears to plunge Antoinette into insanity, but her 'madness' is in truth her violent experience of psychic reorientation. She rejects the European persona Rochester attempts to impose on her, and literally burns it when she sets Thornfield Hall on fire. The infrastructure of the book is in fact a myth – the myth of the Phoenix which destroyed itself to be recreated.[11]

Any such positive interpretation of the book was rejected by Edward Brathwaite in his monograph *Contradictory Omens* (1974). Here Dr Brathwaite argued that Caribbean culture could not be shaped by a meeting of different cultures – such as European and the African. Each individual is conditioned by the 'subjective apprehension of "reality", based upon the particular individual's socio-cultural heritage'.[12] The true Caribbean culture has emerged among the underprivileged West Indian folk by a 'submarine'[13] process of suffering and adaptation. He criticises Look Lai's interpretation of *Wide Sargasso Sea* as offering a delusive prospect of integration between Europe and Africa. He quotes Look Lai on the ending: '[Antoinette's] personal salvation, if it comes at all, will come, not from the destructive alien embrace of Thornfield Hall, but only from a return – however difficult – to the spiritual world on the other side of the Wide Sargasso Sea.' This Dr Brathwaite finds 'hopeful and optimistic, but totally lacking in recognition of the realities of the situation . . . White creoles in the English and French West Indies have separated themselves by too wide a gulf and have contributed too little culturally, as a *group*' for any spiritual identification between white and black. Both the 'cold castle in England' and 'the carefully detailed exotic fantasy of the West Indies' exist only 'inside [Antoinette's] head'.[14]

The analysis, as Kenneth Ramchand has pointed out, 'calls to our notice the danger of prescription that exists whenever we attempt to base definitions upon social and political content'. It might be possible to argue that the book is not in any simple way 'hopeful and optimistic', but that its affirmation of human values lies the far side of the complex difficulties of cultural integration that Dr Brathwaite is anxious to indicate. The novel is a disturbing investigation of the effects of European exploitation against which, in the figure of Christophine, Jean Rhys offers the positive culture of the Caribbean black folk.

Yet such an argument would put the debate about the significance of the novel on a wrong footing. It is validated not by its conformity to any particular viewpoint, but by the depth of its imaginative perception, mediated through the complex experience of the work as a whole. Indeed, as John Hearne asserts, it is the freedom from any conformity that makes *Wide Sargasso Sea* a 'touchstone' for West Indian literature. He couples Jean Rhys with the Guyanese writer Wilson Harris. 'These two alone are free fabulists. They *belong*, but on their own terms. Guerillas, not outsiders.' [15]

Notes

1. Kenneth Ramchand also makes this point, *An Introduction to the Study of West Indian Literature* (1976), pp. 94–96, offering detailed examples.
2. Wally Look Lai, 'The Road to Thornfield Hall' in *New World Quarterly*, Croptime, 1968; reprinted *New Beacon Reviews. Collection One*, ed. John La Rose, 1968
3. Look Lai, *New Beacon Reviews*, p. 40
4. *Ibid.*, p. 52
5. *Contradictory Omens*, pp. 223–231
6. *Ibid.*, p. 225
7. Edgar Mittelholzer, *Children of Kaywana* (1952); *Harrowing of Hubertus* (reissued as *Kaywana Stock*) (1954); *Kaywana Blood* (1958)
8. John Hearne, 'The Wide Sargasso Sea: A West Indian Reflection,' *C.M.*, Summer, 1974, pp. 325–6
9. Hanne Nielsen and Fleming Brahms, 'Retrieval of a Monster: Jean Rhys's *Wide Sargasso Sea*' in K. H. Petersen and A. Rutherford, eds., *Enigma of Values*, Aarhus, Dangeroo Press, 1975, pp. 139–165
10. See, e.g., Wilson Harris, *Fossil and Psyche*, University of Texas, 1974
11. Nielsen and Brahms, pp. 160–1. Even the name, 'Pheena/Phoenix', is connected
12. Brathwaite, *op. cit.*, p. 34
13. *Ibid.*, p. 64
14. *Ibid.*, p. 36
15. Hearne, *op. cit.*, p. 323.

Bibliography

(This list is selective. For a fuller bibliography see Elgin W. Mellown, 'A Bibliography of the Writings of Jean Rhys with a Selected List of Reviews and other Critical Writings', *W.L.W.E*, xvi, 1, April 1977, pp. 179–122.

Works by Jean Rhys

The Left Bank and Other Stories . . . with a Preface by Ford Maddox Ford, Jonathan Cape, London, 1927; Harper and Brothers, New York, 1927.

Postures (also titled *Quartet*), Chatto & Windus, London, 1928; as *Quartet*, Simon and Schuster Inc, New York, 1929; Penguin paperback ed., 1973.

After Leaving Mr. Mackenzie, Jonathan Cape, 1930; Alfred A. Knopf, New York, 1931; Andre Deutsch, 1969; Penguin 1971.

Voyage in the Dark, Whitefriars Press, London, 1934; William Morrow & Co., New York, 1935; Andre Deutsch, 1967; Penguin, 1969.

Good Morning, Midnight, Constable & Co. Ltd., London, 1939; Harper and Row, New York, 1970; Penguin 1969.

Wide Sargasso Sea. Introduction by Francis Wyndham, Andre Deutsch, 1966; W. W. Norton and Co. Inc., New York, 1967; Penguin, 1968.

Tigers are Better-looking, with a Selection from The Left Bank Andre Deutsch, 1968; Penguin, 1973; Harper and Row, New York, 1974.

My Day, Frank Hallman, New York, 1975.

Sleep it Off, Lady, Andre Deutsch, London, 1976; Harper and Row, New York, 1976.

'I spy a Stranger', *Penguin Modern Stories*, I, 1969, pp. 53–68.

'Temps Perdi', *Penguin Modern Stories*, I, 1969, pp. 69–88.

Criticism, biography and reviews

ALVAREZ, A. 'The Best Living English Novelist', *N.Y.T.B.R.*, 17 March 1974, pp. 6–7.

ATHILL, DIANA, 'Jean Rhys and the writing of *Wide Sargasso Sea*', *The Bookseller*, 20 August 1966, pp. 1378–1379.

BOWEN, STELLA, *Drawn from Life* Collins, London, 1941.

BRATHWAITE, EDWARD, *Contradictory Omens*, Mona, Jamaica, 1974, pp. 33–38

BRAYBROOKE, NEVILLE, 'Between Dog and Wolf', *Spectator*, 219, July 21, 1967, 77–8.

'The Return of Jean Rhys', *C.Q.*, December 1970, pp. 43–46.

CANTWELL, MARY, 'I am a Person at a Masked Ball without a Mask . . .' *Mademoiselle*, October 1974, pp. 171–213.

DICK, KAY, '*Wide Sargasso Sea*', *Sunday Times*, 30 October 1966, p. 50.

CASEY FULTON, NANCY J., 'Study in the Alienation of a Creole Woman. Jean Rhys's *Voyage in the Dark*', *C.Q.*, 19 September 1973, pp. 95–102.

'Jean Rhys's *Wide Sargasso Sea*: Exterminating the White Cockroach', *R.I.R.* 4, Fall, 1974, pp. 340–49.

HAMNETT, N., *Laughing Torso*, Constable, London, 1939.

HEARNE, JOHN, '*The Wide Sargasso Sea*: A West Indian Reflection', *C.M.*, Summer 1974, pp. 323–333.

HOPE, FRANCIS, 'Voyage in the Dark and Wide Sargasso Sea', Observer, 11 June 1967, p. 26.

LEWIS, P. WYNDHAM, 'Hinterland of Bohemia', S.R., 143, 23 April 1927, p. 637.

LOOK LAI, WALLY, 'The Road to Thornfield Hall', New Beacon Reviews, ed. John la Rose, London, 1968, pp. 38-52.

LUENGO, ANTHONY E. 'Wide Sargasso Sea and the Gothic Mode', W.L.W.E., 15, April 1976, pp. 229-45.

MELLOWN, ELGIN W., 'Character and Themes in the Novels of Jean Rhys', C.L., 13, 1972, pp. 458-75.

NAIPAUL, V. S., 'Without a Dog's Chance', N.Y.R.B. 18, 18 May, 1872, pp. 29-31.

NIELSEN, HANNE and BRAHMS, FLEMING, 'Retrieval of a Monster: Jean Rhys's Wide Sargasso Sea', in PETERSEN, K. H. and RUTHERFORD, A. eds, Enigma of Values, Aarhus, Denmark, 1975, pp. 139-162.

RAMCHAND, KENNETH, 'Terrified Consciousness', in The West Indian Novel and its Background, Faber, 1970, pp. 223-236.

   'Wide Sargasso Sea', in An Introduction to the Study of West Indian Literature, 1976, pp. 91-107.

RICKS, CHRISTOPHER, 'Female and Other Impersonators', N.Y.R.B., 15, 23 July 1970, pp. 12-13.

THOMAS, NED, 'Meeting Jean Rhys', Planet, August 1976, pp. 29-32.

WILLIAMS, ANGELA, 'The Flamboyant Tree: The World of the Jean Rhys Heroine', Planet, August 1976, pp. 35-41.

'The Left Bank' (review), T.L.S., 5 May 1927, p. 320.

'Postures' (review), T.L.S., 4 October 1928, p. 706.

'The Unholy Four' (review), N.Y.H.T. 10 February 1929, p. 7.

'After Leaving Mr. Mackenzie', (review), T.L.S., 5 March 1931, p. 180.

'Voyage in the Dark', (review), T.L.S., 1 November 1934, p. 752.

'Good Morning Midnight', (review), T.L.S., 12 April 1939, p. 231.

Background to Dominican History

(For a fuller bibliography, see Lennox Honeychurch, below)

ATWOOD, THOMAS, *The History of the Island of Dominica*, London, 1791, repr. Cass, 1971.

CRACKNELL, BASIL, *Dominica*, Newton Abbott, 1973.

DAVY, J. *The West Indies, Before and Wince Slave Emancipation*, W. and G. Cash, London; J. M. Glashan and J. B. Gilpin, Dublin; J. Bowen, Barbados, 1854.

GRIEVE, S. *Notes upon the Island of Dominica*, A. and C. Black, London, 1906.

HONEYCHURCH, LENNOX, *The Dominica Story*, Dominica, 1975.

WAUGH, A., *The Sugar Islands*, New York, 1949.